Images
and
Impressions

Painters
Who
Print

Walker Art Center
23 September to
25 November 1984

Acknowledgments

It has been a privilege to work with the artists in this exhibition. They submitted willing to interviews and were most generous with their time. Our thanks also go to museums, galleries and private individuals who loaned works to this presentation. We appreciate the efforts of the many people who kindly responded to our frequent requests for photographs and information about works of art—among them: Brooke Alexander and Ted Bonin, Brooke Alexander, Inc.; Steven Anderson, Vermillion Editions Ltd.; Russell Bowman, Milwaukee Art Museum; Lynda Forsha, La Jolla Museum of Contemporary Art; Raymond Foye; Ceil Friedman, Barbara Krakow Gallery; Joseph Helman and Judith Hanson, Blum Helman Gallery, Inc.; Antonio Homen and David Nolan, Sonnabend Gallery; Miani Johnson, Willard Gallery; Ulrike Kantor, Ulrike Kantor Gallery; Nathan Kernan, Robert Miller Gallery; Karen McCready and Fredrica Drotos, Crown Point Press; Lynne Sowder, Sowder and Associates; Susan Tallman, Multiples, Inc.; Diane Villani, Diane Villani Editions; Michael Werner, Michael Werner Gallery/Mary Boone Gallery; and Angela Westwater, Sperone Westwater.

We also wish to acknowledge the efforts of the many Walker staff members, listed on page 64, who worked on aspects of this exhibition. In particular, we would like to note the invaluable contribution of Helen Slater, curatorial secretary, and Fiona Irving, curatorial intern, who worked on all aspects of the exhibition's organization. Finally, we thank our director, Martin Friedman, for his support and counsel.
EA & MG

The exhibition *Images and Impressions: Painters Who Print* has been generously supported by a grant from the National Endowment for the Arts. Additional support has come from The McKnight Foundation, the General Mills Foundation, the Bush Foundation, the Dayton Hudson Foundation for B. Dalton Bookseller, Dayton's and Target Stores, and the Minnesota State Arts Board.

In the checklists, height precedes width in inches and in metric measurements. Centimeters are given in parentheses.

Lenders to the Exhibition

Alpha Gallery
Boston, Massachusetts

BankAmerica Corporation Art Collection
San Francisco, California

Brooke Alexander, Inc.
New York, New York

Blum Helman Gallery, Inc.
New York, New York

Mrs. Gustavo Cisneros
Caracas, Venezuela

The Corcoran Gallery of Art
Washington, D. C.

Crown Point Press
Oakland, California and
New York, New York

Dolan/Maxwell Gallery
Philadelphia, Pennsylvania

Gerald S. Elliott
Chicago, Illinois

First Bank Minneapolis
Minneapolis, Minnesota

General Mills Art Collection
Minneapolis, Minnesota

Getler/Pall/Saper Gallery
New York, New York

Ulrike Kantor Gallery
Los Angeles, California

Judy Kay and Associates
San Francisco, California

Galerie & Edition Sabine Knust
New York, New York

La Jolla Museum of Contemporary Art
La Jolla, California

Barbara and Sorrell Mathes
Scarsdale, New York

The Metropolitan Museum of Art
New York, New York

Robert Miller Gallery, Inc.
New York, New York

Milwaukee Art Museum
Milwaukee, Wisconsin

The Minneapolis Institute of Arts
Minneapolis, Minnesota

Multiples, Inc.
New York, New York

Munson-Williams-Proctor Institute
Utica, New York

The Museum of Modern Art
New York, New York

Petersburg Press
New York, New York

Estelle Schwartz
New York, New York

Dr. and Mrs. Mitchell Sheinkop
Chicago, Illinois

T. L. Solien
Pelican Rapids, Minnesota

Sonnabend Gallery
New York, New York

Sperone Westwater
New York, New York

John C. Stoller & Co.
Minneapolis, Minnesota

Romuald Tecco
Minneapolis, Minnesota

Vermillion Editions Ltd.
Minneapolis, Minnesota

Diane Villani Editions
New York, New York

Michael Werner Gallery/
Mary Boone Gallery
New York, New York

Willard Gallery
New York, New York

Four Private Collections

FOREWORD

The title of this exhibition, *Images and Impressions: Painters Who Print,* defines its thesis. These days many artists move easily from one medium to the other, developing thematic and formal ideas in both. Although historically painters have turned to the woodblock, etching plate and lithograph stone to create multiple versions of an idea and so gain greater audiences for their art, until the mid-1960s printmaking in the United States was regarded more as a craft than a medium of invention. Thanks to the relatively recent emergence of a few important print studios, prominent among these Universal Limited Art Editions in Long Island in 1957, Tamarind Workshop in Los Angeles in 1960, Gemini G.E.L. in Los Angeles in 1966 and Tyler Graphics Ltd. in Bedford, New York in 1974, a lively generation of American artists, primarily painters, was introduced to the wonders of graphic processes which it, in turn, vitalized with fresh imagery.

What issued from these workshops forces us to consider printmaking in a new light. Such artists as Robert Motherwell, Jim Dine, Helen Frankenthaler, Jasper Johns, Robert Rauschenberg, Ellsworth Kelly, David Hockney, Frank Stella, Roy Lichtenstein and Claes Oldenburg, working at one or more of these distinguished studios, greatly expanded the range of their expression. Whether working with classic lithography techniques espoused by Tatyana Grosman at ULAE or with high-tech, mixed-media processes encouraged by Kenneth Tyler at his print workshop, these artists were lavishly indulged; at their sides were gifted craftsmen, meticulously trained to help them realize their most ambitious ideas on paper.

After the resurgence of interest in printmaking that began in the 60s, it seemed inevitable that a younger generation of artists would utilize even more complex technology in its printmaking endeavors. While many have immersed themselves in such sophisticated processes, others are revisionists who resort to earlier forms of reproducing images. They prefer carving into wood and linoleum blocks and drawing with tusche crayon on the lithographic stone, or painting with oil pigment on a glass sheet from which a single impression is made.

It is no surprise that revival of interest in such traditional techniques, whether they are practiced in the intimacy of the studio or in a print workshop, should coincide with an international rekindling of interest in realism, primarily the rendering of the human figure. And the dominant mode of such depiction, so evident in recent painting as well as printmaking, is decidedly expressionistic. For all its contemporary spirit, what has been described as "new figuration" and "neo-expressionism" has more than a passing relationship to the moody turbulence of early twentieth-century German Expressionism, with its broadly defined, angular forms and high emotional tension. Other references to recent history are apparent. In some works in this exhibition, a faint haze of Surrealism floats over mystical landscapes. Indeed, such historical stylistic allusions are integral to many images in this presentation, and their use is often ironic, and sometimes rueful. In their hands, déjà vu becomes an aesthetic component.

The Walker Art Center's recent acquisition of the archives of Tyler Graphics Ltd. and their premiere installation in a new wing of the museum were the inspiration for a concurrent exhibition exploring printmaking by a younger generation of artists. This exhibition was developed by two Walker curators, Marge Goldwater and Elizabeth Armstrong, who soon after its initial planning stages, found themselves deeply involved in issues well beyond selecting a group of artists who work both as printmakers and as painters. As their essays in this catalogue—and those of Rainer Crone and Fiona Irving—suggest, in printmaking today many artists are expanding their philosophical and stylistic ranges.   MF

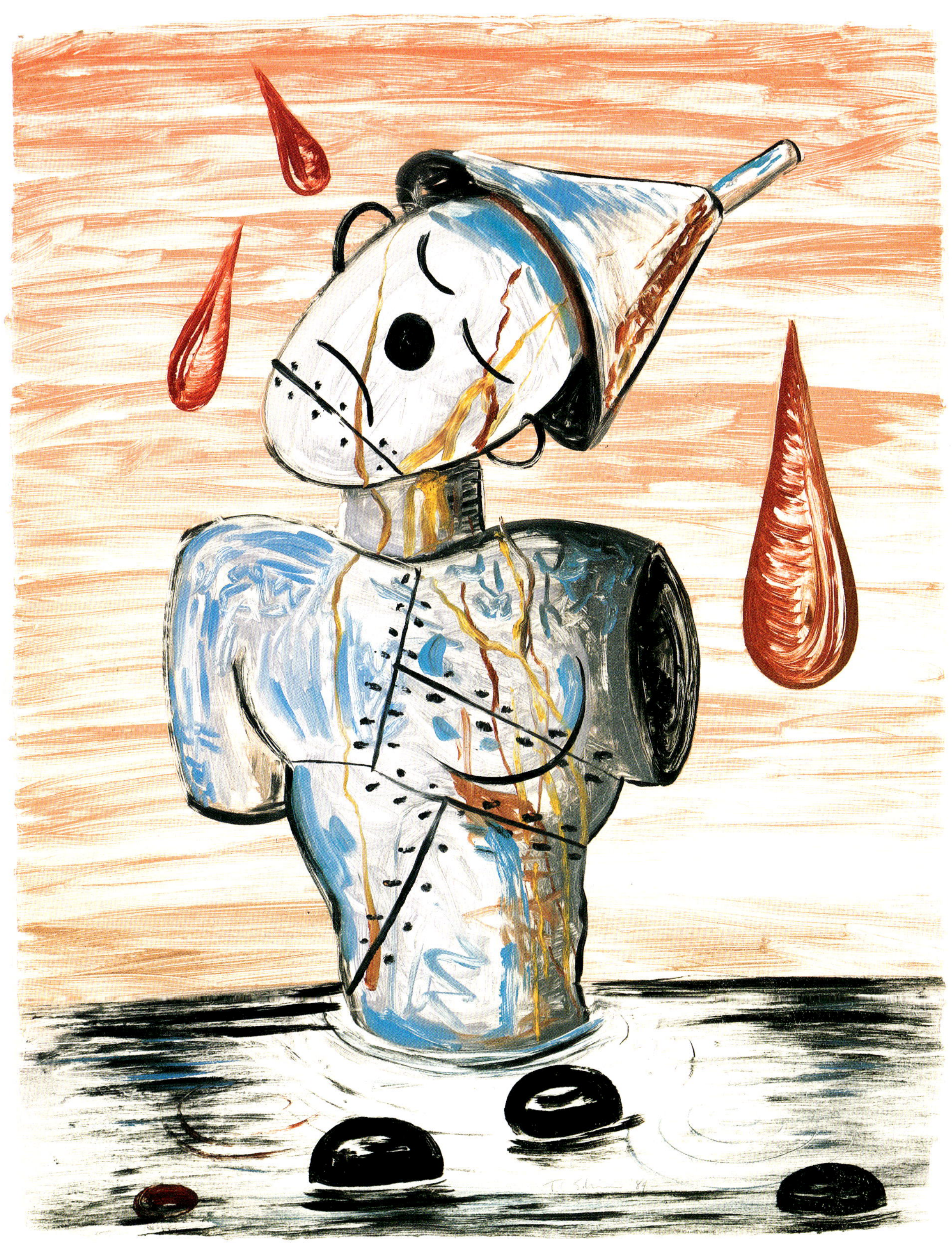

138. T. L. Solien *The Tin Man* 1984

INTRODUCTION

One of the striking phenomena of the current art scene is the increasing interest in printmaking among younger artists here and abroad. More and more artists are turning to the print medium to explore the possibilities of their imagery. As printmaking outgrows its long-held status as the stepchild of the visual arts, its relationship in content and style to other media warrants closer scrutiny. This exhibition is an effort to explore that association, and presents the prints of nine artists in relation to their paintings, drawings and sculpture. Printmaking is integral to the creative processes of these artists; they believe that a healthy cross-fertilization occurs between printmaking and their work in other media. While their individual approaches to printmaking are as varied as their ideas and styles, they share an appreciation of the creative possibilities of the medium.

The nine artists in this exhibition are young. All are in their thirties, the generation that came of age after World War II. Francesco Clemente, Roger Herman, Jörg Immendorff and Mimmo Paladino grew up in Europe; Louisa Chase, Susan Rothenberg, T. L. Solien and Donald Sultan in the United States; and Richard Bosman in Egypt, England and Australia. As many art writers have observed, the apocalyptic undertones of so much recent art is endemic to this generation; no matter where these nine artists spent their early years, they have been affected by the malaise born of fear and uncertainty.[1] Nevertheless, their art is anything but weak and unresponsive to social and personal tensions. While a sense of foreboding is pervasive in much of the work, it is more than matched by vigorous execution and subject matter.

A common thread running throughout this exhibition is the choice of representational imagery as opposed to purely abstract forms. In this respect, the exhibition deals with an especially strong current in art today: an ardent return to the figure. This emphasis on strong figuration clearly distinguishes contemporary artists' production from Minimalism, hard-edge painting, Pop and conceptual art, the dominant artistic movements of the 1960s and 70s. The drama of the self that prevails in this new work was largely rejected by those formalist movements. The realism practiced by these young artists is highly expressive; figures and forms are twisted, distorted and otherwise manipulated to serve as symbols of emotional states. Here and there, stylistic influences from the previous two decades are, nonetheless, discernible. A fascination with the reduction

and dematerialization of forms, for example, is apparent in much of the work. The spirit of Pop, with its ironic recycling of fragments of everyday life, is also in evidence. For the most part, however, their art is less concerned with formalist inquiries or commentary on society's foibles than with highly subjective issues.

This personal quest takes many directions in the work of these nine artists. Immendorff, Bosman and Herman share an interest in early 20th-century German Expressionism, an art full of portent and dire warning about the collapse of society and the futility of individual action in the face of impending disaster. The psychological content of the Expressionists takes on a new immediacy in the social context of Germany today. Growing up in the shadow of World War II, Immendorff is particularly concerned with the psyche of his divided country. He presents an aggressive onslaught of personal, national and media motifs, drawing attention to current historical and political debates with the same fervor as his expressionist forebears. Bosman's figural caricatures, on the other hand, drawn from comic books and B-movies, have an ambivalent detachment that contradicts their desperate narratives as well as their expressionist execution. Herman borrows stylistic elements and subject matter from art history; distorted by their gigantic scale, his mock-heroic paintings and woodcuts of Vincent van Gogh, for example, reflect the artist's attempt to distance himself from his cultural ancestry.

In contrast to the appropriated imagery of Herman and Bosman, Clemente, Paladino and Solien draw from a reservoir of personal symbols. In Solien's narrative compositions, a recurring cast of characters, often featuring the artist as an anxiously staring head, meditate on universal concerns such as the fragility of life and the struggle to maintain one's faith. Paladino's work is an eclectic fusion of dreams and childhood memories steeped in the religious symbolism of his native Italian culture. Phantom figures with elongated mask-like faces haunt the hermetic realm of his prints and paintings. Many of the suspended figures in Clemente's pictures are self-portraits that, dislocated from time and space, seductively invoke a free range of philosophical, allegorical and erotic associations.

While Sultan, Chase and Rothenberg also present figurative imagery in their work, these artists share a preoccupation with the interplay between representation and abstraction. The figurative forms in the work of Chase and Rothenberg are in a constant state of flux as they struggle to emerge from abstract thickets of strokes and markings. Sultan's urban landscapes and still-life images of smokestacks and flowers explore ironic similarities between industrial and natural forms; at the

---

[1] For a few such views, for example, Marcia Tucker's "An Iconography of Recent Figurative Painting: Sex, Death, Violence and the Apocalypse," *Artforum* (New York), Summer 1982, pp. 70–75; Lisa Lyons's *The Anxious Edge*, Walker Art Center, 1982; and Peter Schjeldahl's "Art at the Gates of Hell," *New Figuration in America*, Milwaukee Art Museum, 1982.

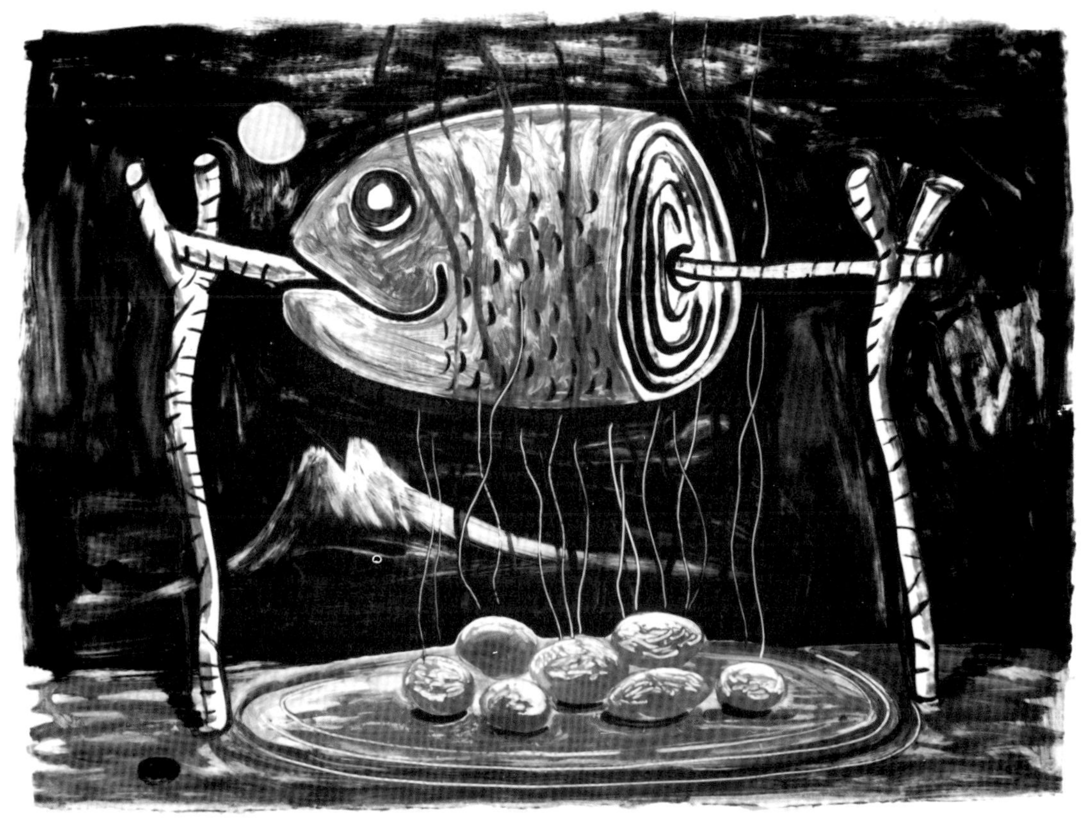

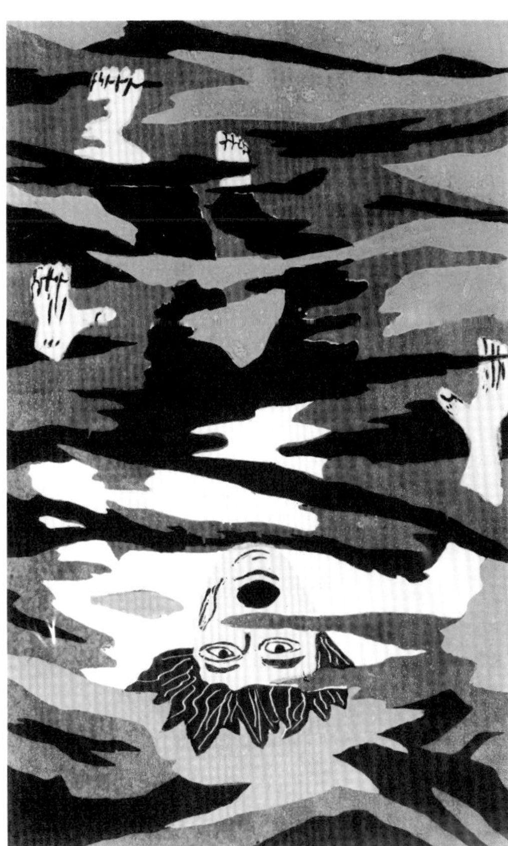

(top)
137.   T. L. Solien
Victim of Doubt   1983

3.   Richard Bosman
Drowning Man I   1981

same time their large fields of color and texture stress the abstract qualities of their structures and shapes.

The richly varied sensibilities of these artists are evident not only in their style and imagery but in the wide range of media they use. Clemente, for instance, has made woodcuts, etchings, monotypes, watercolors, oils, pastels, frescoes, mosaics, photographs, drawings on paper and paintings on just about any available surface from shovels and cement blocks to mirrors, radiators and discarded furniture. Not every artist in this exhibition shares Clemente's physical passion for working with different media, but all have explored their imagery in many forms, on many scales. Immendorff and Paladino, for example, have made monumental, totemlike sculptures hacked out of wood and cast in bronze. On a more intimate scale, many of these artists have created work in book form. Yet a great many of their prints are enormous in size, calling attention to the central importance of the imagery. Bosman's woodcut *The Fall* (1984, no. 25), for example, over five feet high, is larger than many of his paintings, and Herman's immense woodcut *Van Gogh in Red* (1983, no. 66), nine by nine feet, demands to be viewed from a distance.

Unlike the generation that pioneered the American print renaissance in the 1960s and 70s, these younger artists place little emphasis on technical experimentation.[2] At this point, their innovations have more to do with extending their imagery than with technique. In fact, many prefer to work in woodcut, one of printmaking's oldest methods, and with its cruder variant, linocut. In contrast to the technically complex prints that have emerged from the country's leading print workshops over the past two decades, the wood and linocuts of these younger artists are aggressive, even impetuous, reflecting the way they paint and draw. Chase began making woodcuts in response to those of the German Expressionists, and artists with such diverse approaches as Bosman, Herman, Immendorff, Paladino and Rothenberg utilize the character of the wood and linoleum block in a direct manner that also recalls the harsh, angular shapes of Ernst Ludwig Kirchner, Erich Heckel and Emil Nolde. Immendorff's series of ten linocuts called *Café Deutschland gut* (1982–83), based on his paintings in the vast *Café Deutschland* cycle, with particular reference to *Café Deutschland XII– Adlerhälfte*, of 1982, are similarly coarse, revealing qualities particular to this technique. The flat, untextured

surfaces of linoleum restrict the use of tonalities and linear shading, and limit experimentation with additions and omissions. Consequently, Immendorff's *Café Deutschland gut* linocuts, with their solid masses and incisive outlines, are abstracted versions of the paintings; the color variations between each linocut isolate various objects reproduced in each image, further emphasizing the formal qualities of these prints.

Bosman, Clemente, Paladino, Solien and Sultan have all made etchings, taking impressions from the metal plates into which they have spontaneously scratched and scrawled their ideas; technical accidents and fortuitously arrived at marks become part of the animated surfaces of their prints. Responding to questions about his interest in printmaking, Paladino wrote: "I am not interested in the reproducibility, I am fascinated with working on a hostile surface, not knowing what will happen by virtue of the alchemy of the acids." Indeed, Paladino has explored his ideas in a range of print techniques, freely experimenting with etching, drypoint, aquatint and spitbite for various effects in his intaglio prints. The monotype process, which combines painting and printmaking, has been explored by Bosman, Clemente, Immendorff, Rothenberg and Solien. Monotypes are unique images taken from the plate, usually glass or plexiglass, on which the artist has directly painted. Solien, who may spend a month making a painting, is attracted to the immediacy of the monotype process, which requires the artist to work rapidly since the image must be printed while the paint or ink is still wet. Working in monotype, Solien has produced some of his most gruesome and uninhibited imagery to date. Bosman, who once used linocuts as drawings for his early paintings, now often finds that ideas first occuring in his monotypes subsequently metamorphose into paintings and woodcuts.

Although the print workshop provides a collaborative atmosphere very different from the isolation of the painting studio, printmaking is a creative stimulus much like painting for these artists. The aggressive digging and gouging required to make wood and linocuts, the biting force of the acid used in etching, and the gestural spontaneity afforded by the monotype are invigorating physical processes that offer formal and technical challenges. Ideas that begin in one medium are often carried into another by these artists, and a dialogue exists between these vital aspects of their production. Printmaking for them is not merely a reproduction of their painting ideas into another technique, but offers new ways of thinking and working. In their art, it is anything but afterthought; it is a central means of expression.   EA

2   Jasper Johns, Robert Rauschenberg, Roy Lichtenstein, Ellsworth Kelly and Frank Stella, for example, were challenged by the possibility of extending technical processes of the graphic media beyond known limitations. Many of these artists are featured in the concurrent exhibition at Walker Art Center, *Prints from Tyler Graphics*.

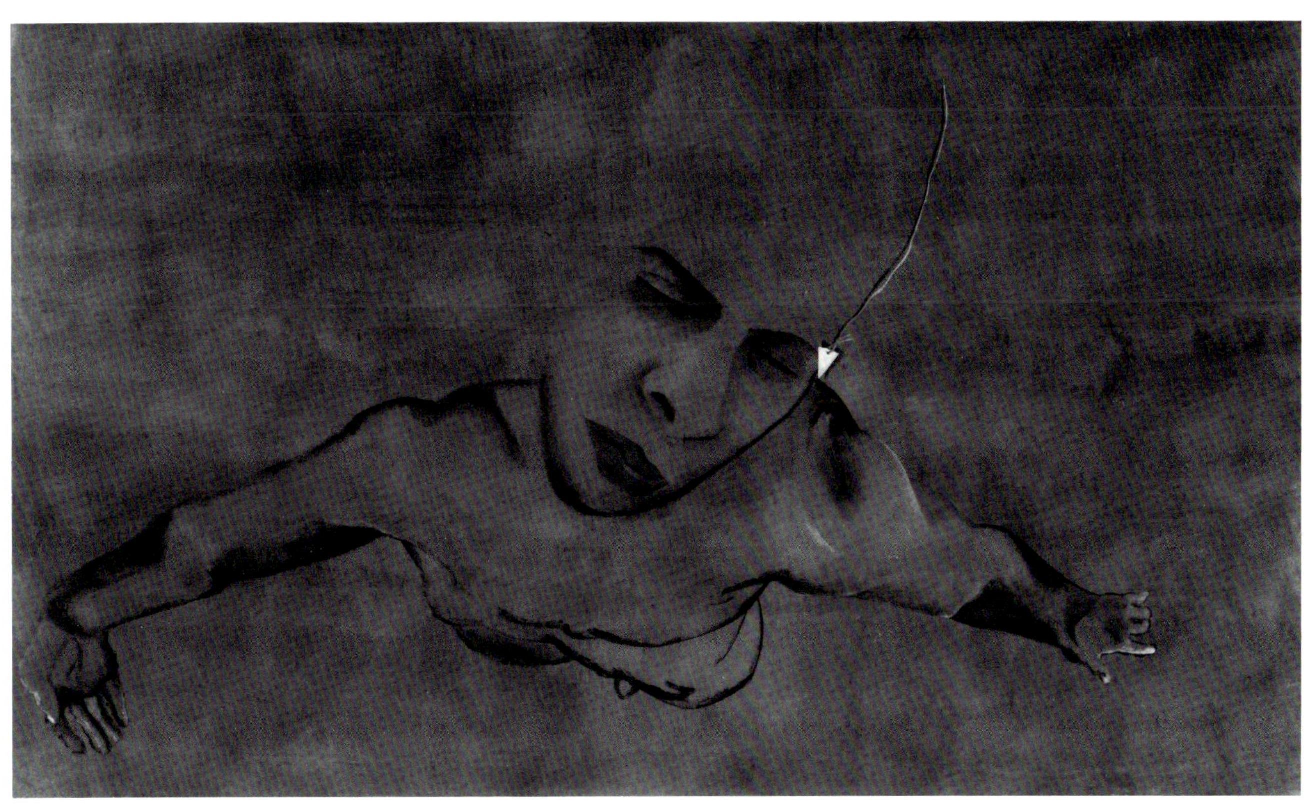

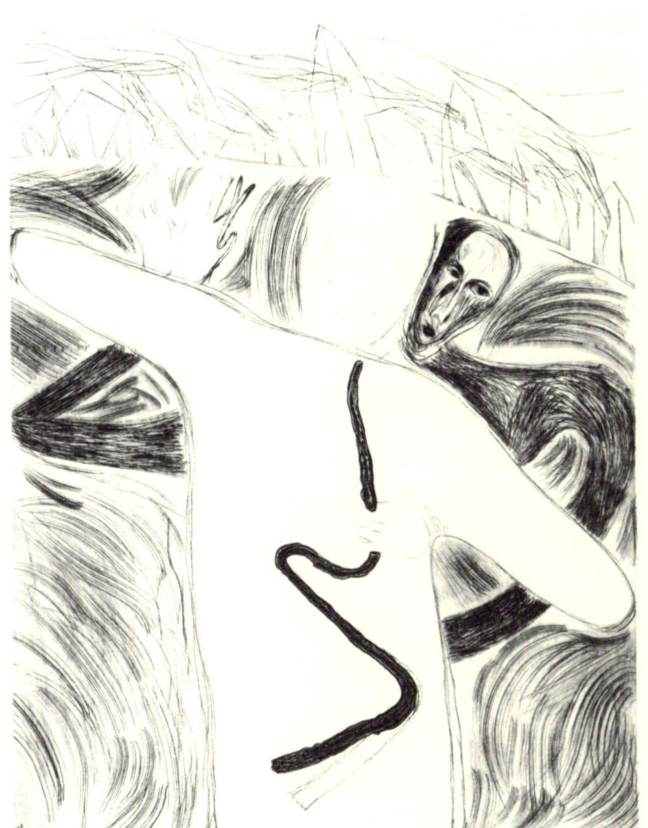

(top)
46.   Francesco Clemente
Semen   1983

86.   Mimmo Paladino
Figure Semplici   1982

RICHARD BOSMAN

Clinging to the hull of a capsized boat, wrestling a polar bear, or plummeting headfirst into the void of sea or sky, Richard Bosman's figures inhabit a threatening world of danger and suspense. These unfortunate victims are incongruously depicted, however, in a humorously simplified fashion. Reduced to caricature, their flat, paper-doll-like forms have a lifeless complacency that completely contradicts their desperate straits. The lassitude of these figures is contradicted not only by their perilous circumstances but by the vehement manner in which they are depicted. The slashing, jagged gouges of Bosman's woodcuts and the frantic, thick brushstrokes of his paintings are pure expressionist execution, leading us to expect a heavy load of subjectivity and emotionality, which is not to be found in his art.

While the subject and tone of Bosman's art is radically different from that of early 20th-century German Expressionists, he shares their style of execution and their love of the graphic medium. Over the past few years, Bosman has continually used the printmaking process to work out ideas and compositions. His earliest prints were linocuts, to which he attributes the predominance of night imagery in his work. He left the backgrounds of his linoleum blocks uncut so they always printed black, suggesting nocturnal vignettes. Since 1981, Bosman has been extensively exploring woodcut technique with masterly results, and has tried his hand at etching and stencil printing as well. He also works with the spontaneous monotype process, and the resulting images have served as identifiable sources for subsequent paintings and prints.

The son of a Dutch sea captain, Bosman grew up in such exotic cities as Madras, Suez, Singapore and Perth. He has made several long ocean voyages and in his subject matter often uses sea themes. Since 1969, he has lived in New York City, and the metropolis is now a frequent setting in his work. His imagery also derives from popular culture–the mass media, detective stories, B-movies, television news and comic books have all supplied ideas. He says his first figurative works were directly influenced by Asian comic books he picked up in New York's Chinatown.

Bosman's first woodcut, *Man Overboard* (1981, no. 4), combined autobiographical sources with those from popular culture. Its lugubrious theme was inspired by a childhood memory of an ocean voyage from Australia to England when a priest threw himself overboard. Bosman specifically remembers that the priest left his shoes on the ship's deck. If the print originated in personal incident, its composition showing a man plunging to his death came, the artist says, from the cover of a detective story.

Bosman's virtually flat, cartoon-like rendering of people like the barefoot jumper in *Man Overboard* is to some extent a mimicry of mass-media sources. At the same time, his free distortion of the human figure places emphasis on arresting formal aspects of his compositions. His method of flattening his figures so that they are part of the picture's depth recalls the paintings of Alex Katz, under whom he studied at the New York Studio School when he first moved to the city.

Such formalistic qualities in Bosman's work are, however, often overwhelmed by the sheer force of his imagery. His transmutation of characters from popular culture into heroic subjects of large-scale paintings and prints presents the viewer with an intriguing, but unsettling incongruity; the mixture of humor and menace in his work is equally disconcerting. Often faced with life-and-death situations, Bosman's anonymous figures are disconnected from their surroundings; they exist, rather, in a subconscious realm, a shadowy area of impulses, obsessions and fears.

In the 1983 woodcut *Survivor* (no. 22), another of Bosman's phantoms appears. Crudely silhouetted against a dark sky swept by arcs of light, this lone figure might be fleeing from any number of scenarios–from a pulp fiction villain to a nuclear holocaust. While the viewer may share Bosman's facetious attitude toward either of these clichés, he or she cannot escape an underlying feeling of apprehension. No matter how corny or cosmic, Bosman's characters, set in situations beyond their control, mirror the anxiety that prevails in society. Their benumbed response to the threatening environment is disturbingly familiar. Taking a fatalistic view of a perilous world, Bosman's expressionless expressionism is exceedingly of its time.   EA

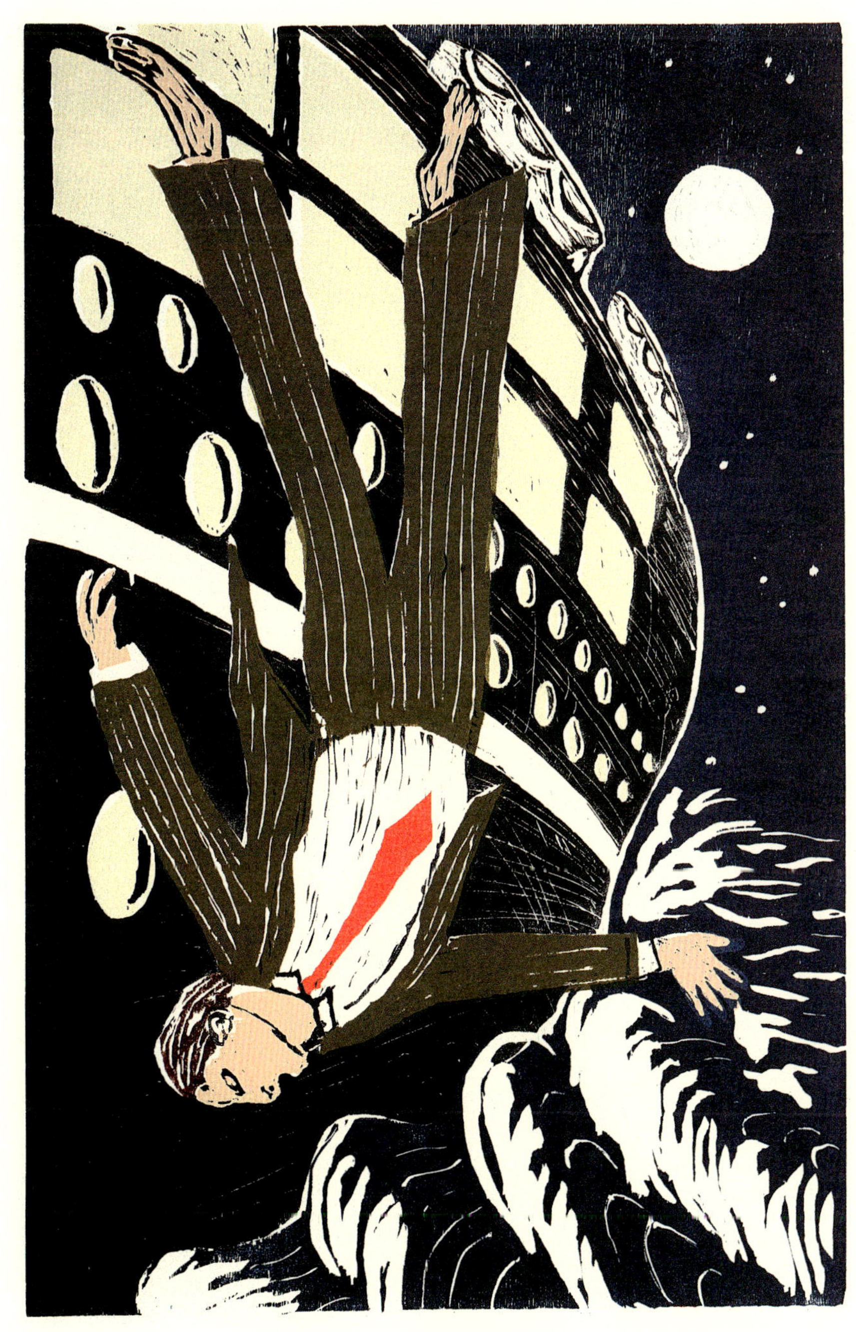

4. *Man Overboard* 1981

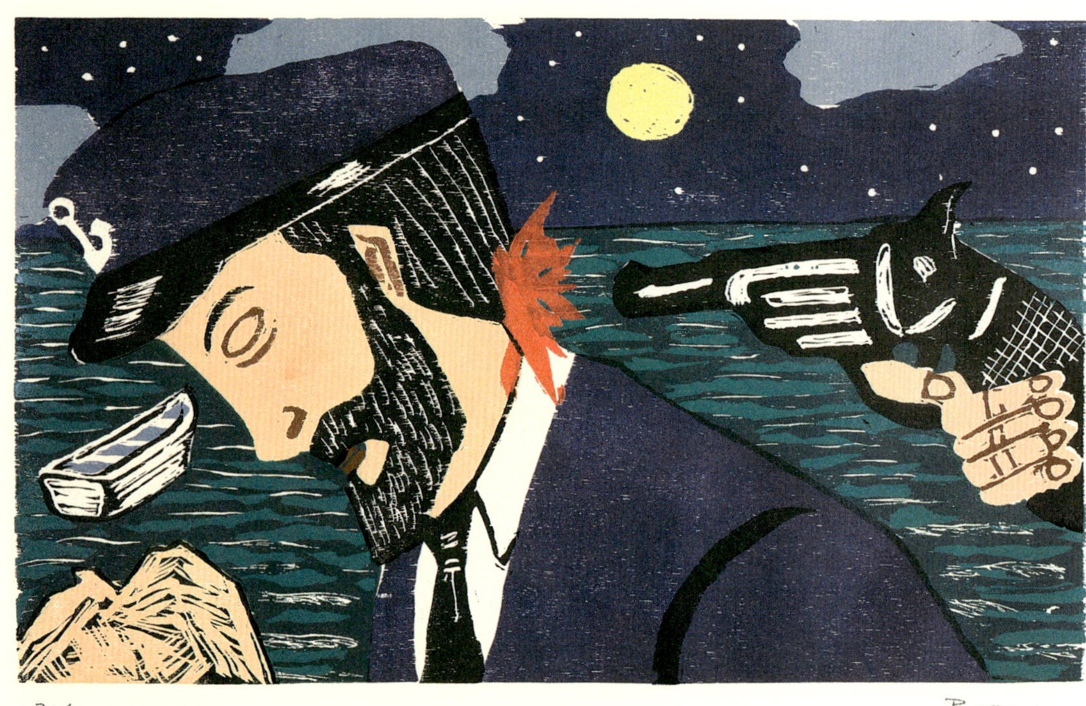

5. *Mutiny* 1981

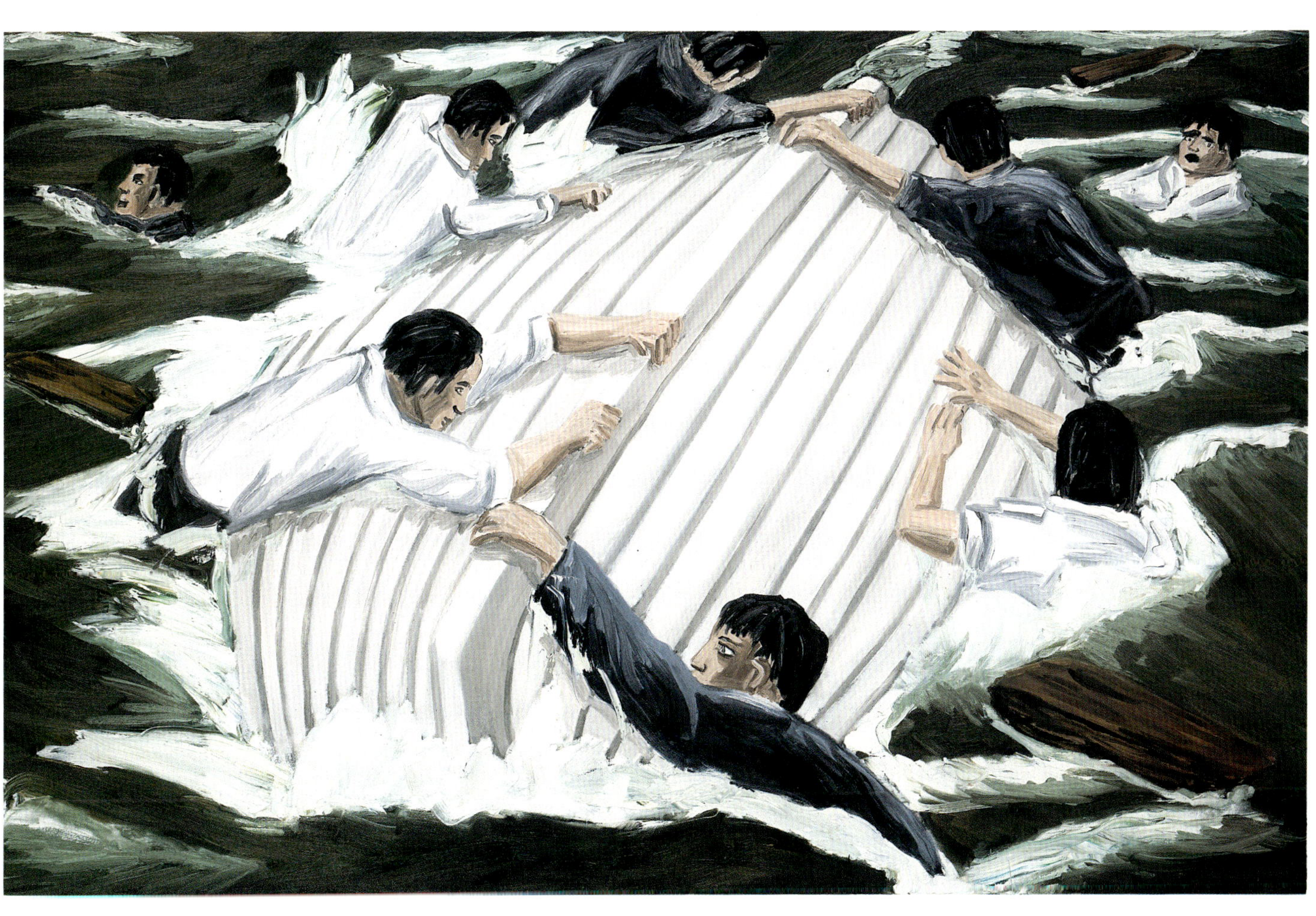

2. *Capsized* 1982

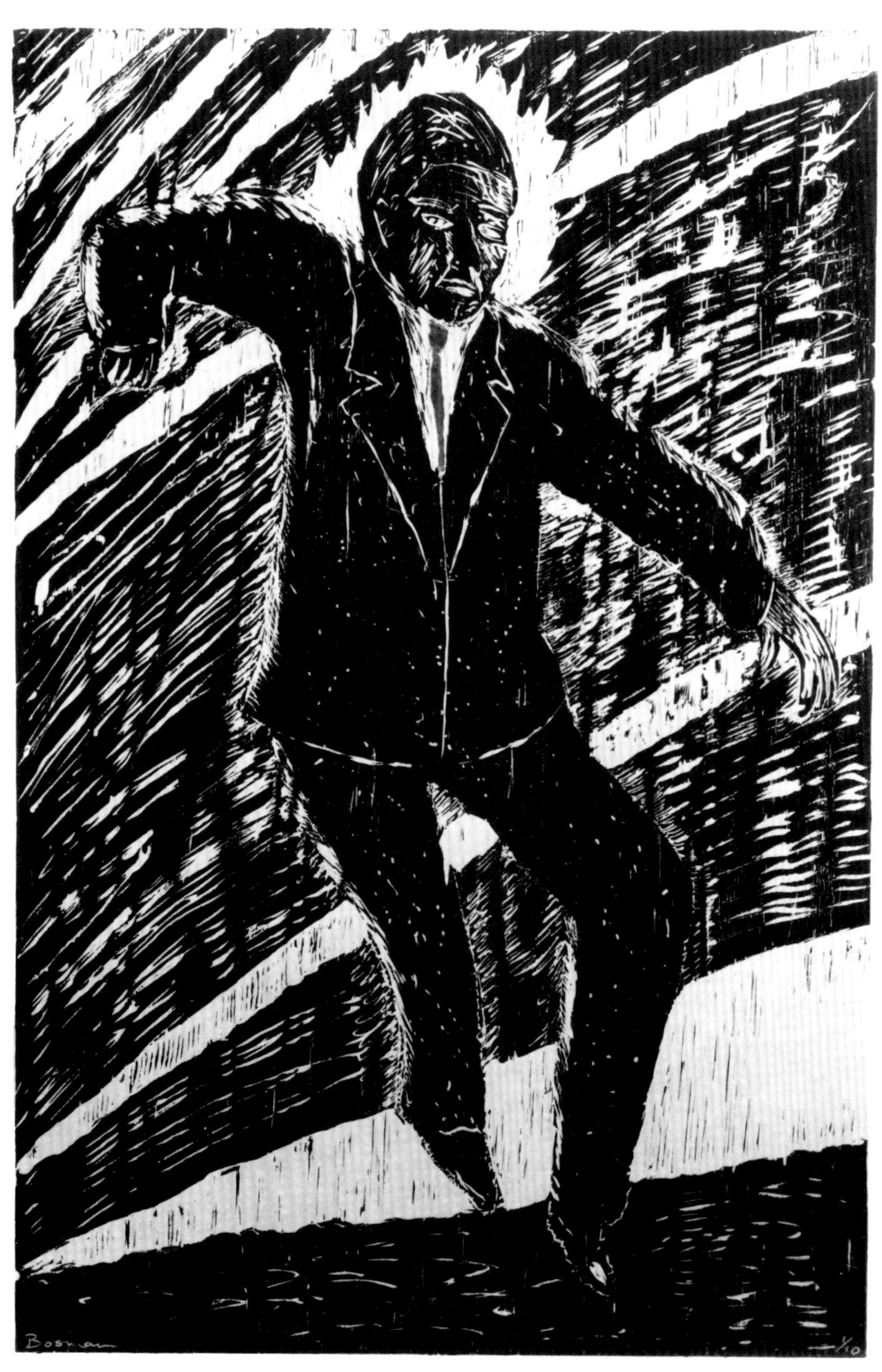

22. *Survivor* 1983

RICHARD BOSMAN

1944
Born in Madras, India
1964–69
Attended the Byam Shaw School of Painting
and Drawing, London
1969–71
Attended the New York Studio School
Lives in New York

Solo Exhibitions
1980
Brooke Alexander, Inc., New York
1981
Brooke Alexander, Inc., New York
1982
Thomas Segal Gallery, Boston
Dart Gallery, Chicago
Brooke Alexander, Inc., New York
Focus: Richard Bosman,
The Fort Worth Art Museum (brochure)
1983
Brooke Alexander, Inc., New York
Reconnaissance, Melbourne, Australia
Mayor Gallery, London
1984
Brooke Alexander, Inc., New York

Selected Group Exhibitions
1980
The Times Square Show, Times Square,
New York
Selections 11, The Drawing Center,
New York
Illustration and Allegory,
Brooke Alexander, Inc., New York
1981
*Body Language: Figurative Aspects of
Recent Art,* Hayden Gallery, Massachusetts
Institute of Technology, Cambridge
(catalogue)
For Love and Money: Dealer's Choice, Pratt
Manhattan Center Gallery, New York
(catalogue)
Twenty-second National Print Exhibition,
The Brooklyn Museum, New York
(catalogue)
1982
New Drawing in America, The Drawing
Center, New York (catalogue)
Block Prints, Whitney Museum of American
Art, New York (brochure)
Focus on the Figure: Twenty Years, Whitney
Museum of American Art, New York
(catalogue)
Awards in the Visual Arts,
National Museum of American Art,
Washington, D.C. (catalogue)
74th American Exhibition, The Art Institute
of Chicago (catalogue)
Painting and Sculpture Today 1982,
Indianapolis Museum of Art (catalogue)
New Figuration in America,
Milwaukee Art Museum (catalogue)
The Image Scavengers, Institute of
Contemporary Art, University of
Pennsylvania, Philadelphia (catalogue)
Beasts, The Institute for Art and Urban
Resources, P.S. 1, Long Island City,
New York (brochure)

1983
Monotypes, The Neuberger Museum,
State University of New York, Purchase
Prints from Blocks: Gauguin to Now,
The Museum of Modern Art, New York
(catalogue)
*The American Artist as Printmaker:
Twenty-third National Print Exhibition,*
The Brooklyn Museum, New York
(catalogue)
1984
*The End of the World: Contemporary
Visions of the Apocalypse,* The New
Museum of Contemporary Art, New York
(catalogue)
Victims and Violations, The Contemporary
Arts Center, New Orleans (brochure)
*Paradise Lost/Paradise Regained: American
Visions of the New Decade,*
Venice Biennale, American Pavilion
*An International Survey of Recent Painting
and Sculpture,* The Museum of Modern Art,
New York (catalogue)
The Human Condition: Biennale III,
San Francisco Museum of Modern Art
(catalogue)

CHECKLIST

Paintings
1. *Adversaries* 1981
oil on canvas
72⅛ x 42 (183 x 106.6)
Collection The Museum of Modern Art,
New York
Gift of Mr. and Mrs. Carl D. Lobell, 1982
2. *Capsized* 1982
oil on canvas
72 x 108 (182.9 x 274.3)
Collection The Metropolitan Museum
of Art, New York
Gift of Mr. and Mrs. Wilson Nolen

Prints
3. *Drowning Man I* 1981
woodcut on paper; edition: 30
image: 40 x 23¾ (101.6 x 60.3)
sheet: 47½ x 30 (120.7 x 76.2)
General Mills Art Collection, Minneapolis
4. *Man Overboard* 1981
woodcut on paper; edition: 36
image: 23¾ x 15 (60.3 x 38.1)
sheet: 26⅝ x 16¼ (67.6 x 41.3)
Courtesy Brooke Alexander, Inc.,
New York
5. *Mutiny* 1981
woodcut on paper; edition: 36
image: 15 x 24 (38.1 x 61)
sheet: 18¾ x 24¾ (47.6 x 62.9)
Collection Mr. and Mrs. Wilson Nolen,
New York
Courtesy Brooke Alexander, Inc.
6. *Polar Bear* 1981
woodcut on paper; edition: 14
image: 23¾ x 22 (60.3 x 55.9)
sheet: 30 x 25½ (76.2 x 64.8)
Private Collection
Courtesy Brooke Alexander, Inc.,
New York

7. *South Sea Kiss* 1981
woodcut on paper; edition: 31
image: 15 x 23⅜ (38.1 x 59.4)
sheet: 16¼ x 24½ (41.3 x 62.2)
Collection Mr. and Mrs. Wilson Nolen,
New York
Courtesy Brooke Alexander, Inc.,
New York
8. *Suicide* 1981
woodcut on paper; edition: 42
sheet and image: 13¼ x 27½ (33.7 x 69.9)
Courtesy Brooke Alexander, Inc.,
New York
9. *Adversaries* 1982
woodcut on paper; edition: 42
image: 30 x 19⅞ (76.2 x 50.5)
sheet: 30½ x 20½ (77.5 x 52.1)
Collection Carl and Katherine Lobell,
New York
Courtesy Brooke Alexander, Inc.,
New York
10. *Nightmare* 1983
etching, hand-colored with watercolor,
on paper; edition: 20
image: 11¾ x 17⅞ (29.8 x 45.4)
sheet: 22¾ x 29½ (57.8 x 74.9)
Courtesy Brooke Alexander, Inc.,
New York
11. *Night Visitor* 1983
woodcut on paper; edition: 35
image: 24⅜ x 25¼ (61.9 x 64.1)
sheet: 25 x 25¼ (63.5 x 64.1)
Courtesy Brooke Alexander, Inc.,
New York
12. *Revenge of the Cat* 1983
etching on paper; edition: 40
image: 2 plates, each 23⅝ x 17¾
(60 x 45.1)
sheet: 31⅛ x 43¼ (79 x 109.9)
Courtesy Brooke Alexander, Inc.,
New York
13–21. *Survivor* 1983
woodcuts on paper; nine color trial proofs
image: 38 x 23⅞ each (96.5 x 60.6)
sheet: 39¼ x 24⅞ each (99.7 x 64.8)
Courtesy Brooke Alexander, Inc.,
New York
22. *Survivor* 1983
woodcut on paper; edition: 10
image: 38 x 23⅞ (96.5 x 60.6)
sheet: 39¼ x 24⅞ (99.7 x 64.8)
Courtesy Brooke Alexander, Inc.,
New York
23. *Life Raft* 1983–84
etching on paper; edition: 40
sheet and image: 22 x 29½ (55.9 x 74.9)
Courtesy Brooke Alexander, Inc.,
New York
24. *The Rescue* 1983–84
woodcut on paper; edition: 32
sheet and image: 38 x 50 (96.5 x 127)
Courtesy Brooke Alexander, Inc.,
New York
25. *The Fall* 1984
woodcut on paper; edition: 32
image: 56½ x 41½ (143.5 x 105.4)
sheet: 60½ x 41½ (153.7 x 105.4)
Courtesy Brooke Alexander, Inc.,
New York

LOUISA CHASE

In Louisa Chase's visions of nature, fires, blizzards, sunsets and squalls rage across the landscape. Nature is never static in her atmospheric images, which range from the turbulent to the transcendent. Her palette of lurid pinks and mauves, throbbing reds and oranges, vibrant blues and greens is intensified by the heavy layers of brushstrokes on her canvases and the spirited markings in her woodcuts. Often, these psychic landscapes are inhabited by fragments of human figures–torsos, hands, and feet–that draw us into their inner sanctum. These enigmatic fragments provide constant reference to the artist's presence, and the rawness of their naked forms adds a disquieting sensuality to the already feverish quality of these compositions.

Like many young artists today, Chase feels a deep affinity with the mystical landscapes of early American modernists such as Arthur Dove and Georgia O'Keeffe and with the emotional dramas that occur in German Expressionist paintings and prints. When she saw the exhibition *Expressionism: A German Intuition 1905–1920* at The Solomon R. Guggenheim Museum, New York, in 1980, she was particularly struck by the power of the woodcuts. Soon, she started to explore the medium on her own, her first foray into printmaking after leaving art school. Two black and white woodcuts, *Cave* and *Squall* (1981, nos. 29, 30) began with preparatory drawings that Chase tranferred directly to the blocks. She became increasingly fascinated with the woodcutting process and with the character of markings that resulted from manipulation of the hand tools. Her original concepts for the prints fell away as she let her involvement with the carving process dictate the forms of the finished works.

One reason the woodcut process so intrigued Chase was that it forced her to cut into and thus animate the large, solid forms that she favored during this period. Her tendency to shape imagery out of large, blocklike masses is evident in a 1983 print titled *Chasm* (no. 34). In this work, a pair of gently rendered feet rests at the edge of a jagged precipice, animated by surrounding cliffs that jut into each other at all angles. In her paintings of the early 1980s, these same forms are presented as dense and weighty. In her prints, they have less materiality–they are simultaneously opaque and atmospheric.

The woodcut experience of "lightening" form through activating its surface was to have a significant effect on Chase's painting, stimulating her to think anew about the relationship of solid forms to voids in her work. She became increasingly interested in energizing space in her compositions. While her earlier interest, she says, was the shallow "invented" space of early Renaissance art, particularly the Siennese school, she now prefers the more "experiential" space of the abstract expressionists, especially the infinite space envisaged by Jackson Pollock. In Chase's recent works, disembodied figures like the wonderful, mute feet in *Chasm* no longer hover in the landscape; rather, she says, the space now fills the figure. Intensely palpable, the space is charged by markings like particles in a wild energy field. In *The Passing* (1983–84, no. 27), for example, phantomlike hands reverberate with impulsive markings that activate the space of the picture as never before.

While the woodblock technique was easily adapted to Chase's incisive delineation of forms in her earlier work, her heightened interest in space and in process has now led her to make etchings. This venerable print technique, with its great range of tonality and textural possibilities, seems ideal for an artist who is increasingly interested in representing force and movement through abstract form. In the etchings, shapes have become less delineated and more vaporous, with individual strokes and marks more prominent. The disembodied torso and fluttering hands in the untitled print of 1984 (no. 37), for instance, struggle to materialize from a frenzy of etched lines and aquatint washes, suggesting transformation and growth.

As Chase strives to translate her visual language into dynamic gesture, her work has taken on a more intuitive and less descriptive aspect. As she puts it, these are statements about feelings, not things: "The physicality of the work, of the gesture, is so much closer to the uncontrollability of the feeling than a symbolic depiction." There is something almost primal about the deliberate formlessness of Chase's recent work as parts of human figures become co-extensive with the forces of nature. Intensely expressionistic, her anxious search to express emotional states and intensities of feeling is communicated with a physical urgency.　　EA

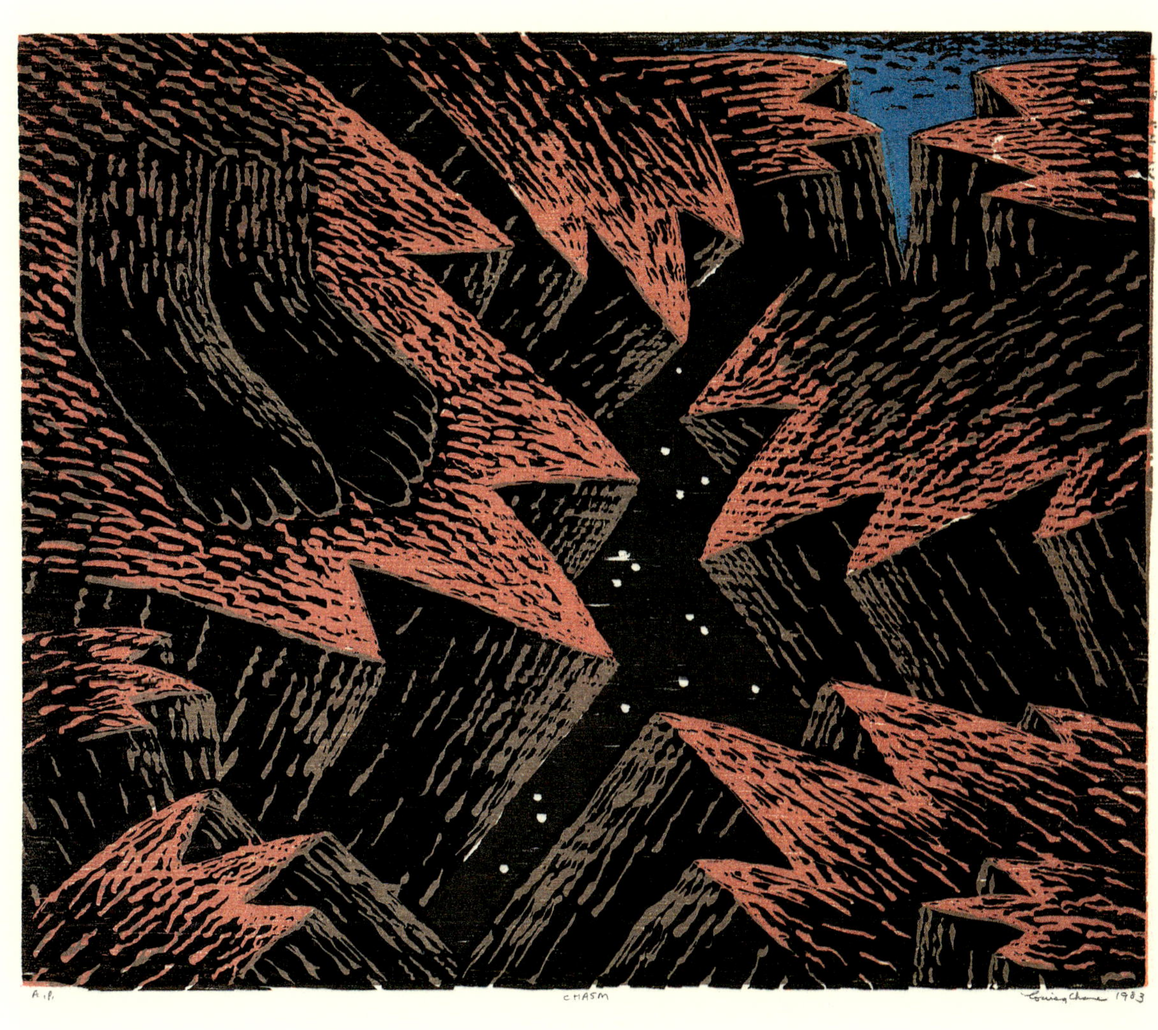

34. *Chasm* 1983

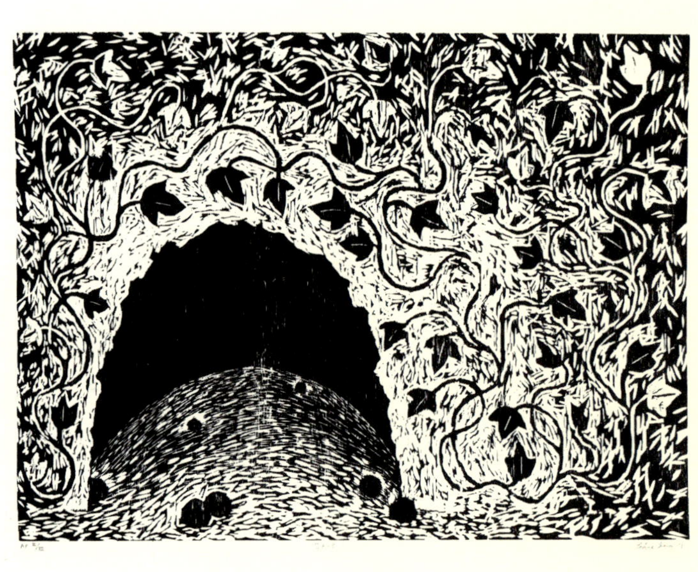

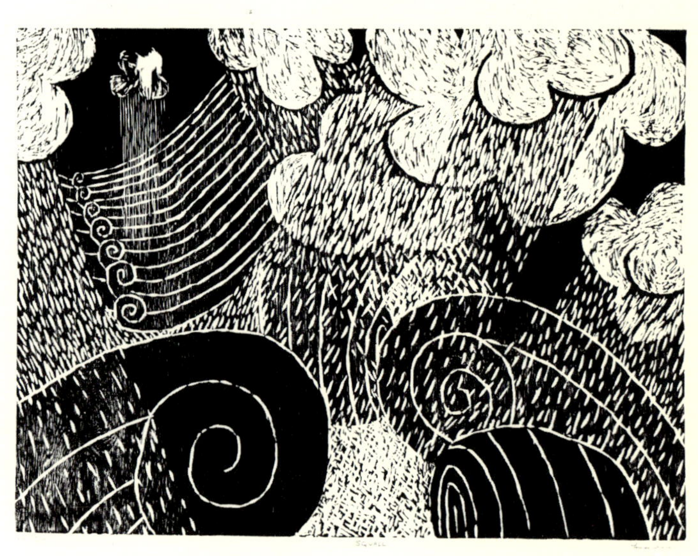

29. *Cave* 1981 (top)
30. *Squall* 1981

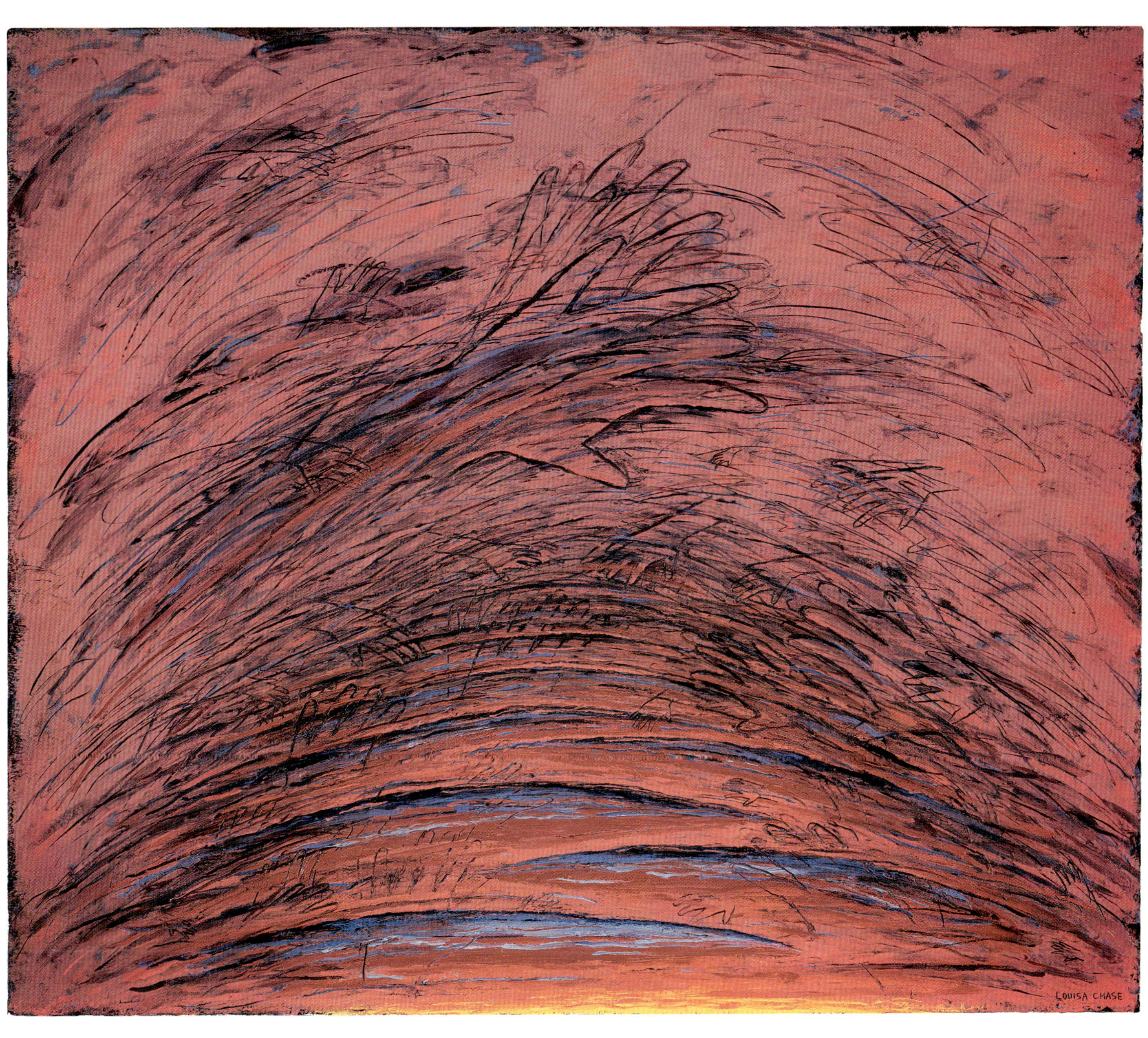

27. *The Passing*   1983 – 84

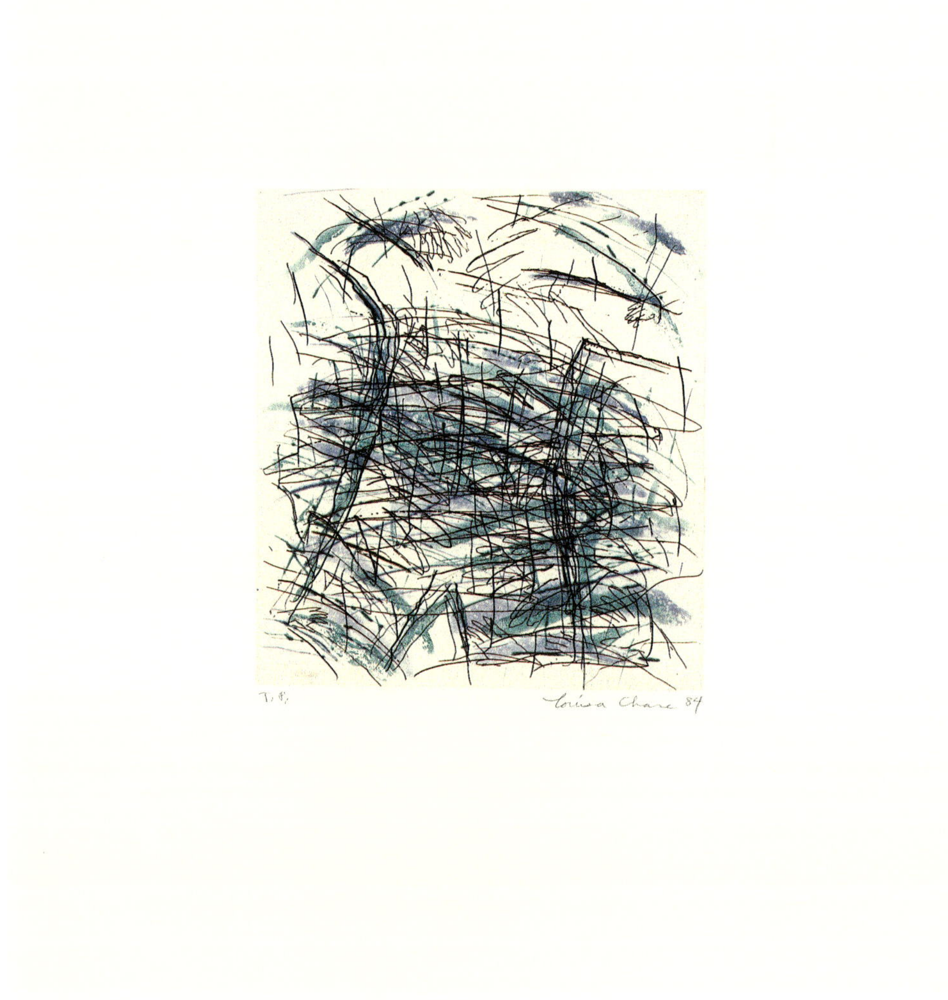

37. Untitled (*Water*) 1984

LOUISA CHASE

1951
Born in Panama City, Panama
1971
B.F.A., Syracuse University, Syracuse,
New York
1975
M.F.A., Yale University School of Art,
New Haven, Connecticut
Lives in New York

Solo Exhibitions
1975
Artists Space, New York
1978
Edward Thorp Gallery, New York
1981
Robert Miller Gallery, New York
1982
Robert Miller Gallery, New York
Harcus-Krakow Gallery, Boston
1983
Galerie Inge Baeker, Cologne,
West Germany
1984
Robert Miller Gallery, New York
(catalogue)
Mira Godard Gallery, Toronto

Selected Group Exhibitions
1979
American Painting: The Eighties, Grey Art
Gallery, New York University, New York.
Traveled to Contemporary Arts Museum,
Houston (catalogue)
1980
New Work/New York, The New Museum,
New York (catalogue)
Painting and Sculpture Today 1980,
Indianapolis Museum of Art (catalogue)
1981
New Visions, Aldrich Museum of
Contemporary Art, Ridgefield, Connecticut
(catalogue)
1981 Biennial Exhibition, Whitney
Museum of American Art, New York
(catalogue)
1982
Painting and Sculpture Today 1982,
Indianapolis Museum of Art (catalogue)
Zeichnung Heute, Kunsthalle Nürnberg,
West Germany. Traveled to Musée
Cantonal des Beaux-Arts, Lausanne,
Switzerland (catalogue)
Block Prints, Whitney Museum of American
Art, New York (brochure)
1983
Back to the U.S.A., Kunstmuseum Luzern,
Lucerne, Switzerland. Traveled to
Rheinisches Landesmuseum, Bonn,
West Germany; Württembergischer
Kunstverein, Stuttgart, West Germany
(catalogue)
*The American Artist as Printmaker:
Twenty-third National Print Exhibition,*
The Brooklyn Museum, New York
(catalogue)

1984
*New Vistas: Contemporary American
Landscapes,* The Hudson River Museum,
Yonkers, New York (catalogue)
New Narrative Painting, The Metropolitan
Museum of Art (catalogue)
*Paradise Lost/Paradise Regained: American
Visions of the New Decade,* Venice
Biennale, American Pavilion
*An International Survey of Recent Painting
and Sculpture,* The Museum of Modern Art,
New York (catalogue)

CHECKLIST

Paintings
26. *Crevasse* 1982
oil on canvas
60 x 72 (152.4 x 182.9)
Private Collection
27. *The Passing* 1983 – 84
oil on canvas
84 x 96 (231.4 x 243.8)
Collection The Corcoran Gallery of Art,
Washington, D.C.
Gift of the Women's Committee of
The Corcoran Gallery of Art

Drawings
28. Untitled 1981
charcoal, pastel on paper
48 x 101 (121.9 x 256.5)
Courtesy Robert Miller Gallery, New York

Prints
29. *Cave* 1981
woodcut on paper; edition: 15
image: 30 x 40 (76.2 x 101.6)
sheet: 37⅜ x 46¼ (94.9 x 117.5)
Courtesy Diane Villani Editions, New York
30. *Squall* 1981
woodcut on paper; edition: 20
image: 30 x 40 (76.2 x 101.6)
sheet: 37⅜ x 45⅞ (94.9 x 116.5)
Courtesy Diane Villani Editions, New York
31. *Dawn* 1982
woodcut on paper; edition: 20
image: 24 x 48 (61 x 121.9)
sheet: 29 x 52¼ (74.7 x 132.7)
Courtesy Diane Villani Editions, New York
32. *Dusk* 1982
woodcut on paper; edition: 20
image: 24 x 48 (61 x 121.9)
sheet: 29 x 52¼ (74.7 x 132.7)
Courtesy Diane Villani Editions, New York
33. *Black Sea* 1983
woodcut on paper; edition: 25
sheet and image: 29¾ x 35⅞ (75.6 x 90.6)
Courtesy Diane Villani Editions, New York
34. *Chasm* 1983
woodcut on paper; edition: 30
image: 24 x 28 (61 x 71.1)
sheet: 26⅛ x 30⅛ (66.4 x 76.5)
Courtesy Diane Villani Editions, New York
35. *Red Sea* 1983
woodcut on paper; edition: 25
sheet and image: 33 x 38¾ (83.8 x 98.4)
Courtesy Diane Villani Editions, New York

36. Untitled *(Fire)* 1984
etching, spit bite, drypoint on paper;
edition: to be determined
image: 7⅜ x 9¾ (18.7 x 24.8)
sheet: 18½ x 19¾ (47 x 50.2)
Courtesy Diane Villani Editions, New York
37. Untitled *(Water)* 1984
etching, spit bite, drypoint on paper;
edition: to be determined
image: 7¾ x 7⅛ (19.7 x 18.1)
sheet: 18⅞ x 15⅛ (47.9 x 38.4)
Courtesy Dianc Villani Editions, New York
38 – 43. Untitled 1984
portfolio of six etchings with spit bite,
drypoint on paper; edition: to be determined
four images: 5 x 6 each (12.7 x 15.2)
two images: 6 x 5 each (15.2 x 12.7)
sheet: 11⅛ x 11 each (28. 3 x 27.9)
Courtesy Diane Villani Editions, New York
44. *Woods* 1984
etching, spit bite, drypoint on paper;
edition: to be determined
image: 23¾ x 25¼ (60.3 x 64.1)
sheet: 31⅞ x 31½ (81 x 80)
Courtesy Diane Villani Editions, New York

FRANCESCO CLEMENTE

The Sirens. Yes, they really sang, but not in a very
satisfactory way. Their song merely suggested the
direction from which the perfect song might come. Yet
through their perfect song–a song as yet unborn–they
lured the navigator towards the space where singing
really begins. . .
Maurice Blanchot, *The Song of the Sirens*

In 1981, Neapolitan painter Francesco Clemente, on his
way from Madras, India, where from 1974 he had been
spending three or four months a year, to New York City,
his present home, stopped at the Crown Point Press in
Oakland, California. There the young conceptual artist
executed for the first time a series of "conventional"
prints including his series of self-portraits (nos. 51–53)
and the oversize aquatint etching *Not St. Girolamo*
(no. 50).

Interviewed soon after, Clemente stated that the
prints were not translations of his other work: "I never
surrendered to the idea that I am a painter. Therefore
everything I do . . . for the first time [is] a thing in itself.
I try . . . not [to reelaborate] previous images. The frame
given me by the etching–its limits–makes me think of new
images . . . new inspirations."

In fact *Not St. Girolamo* is for Clemente a new
image and a new inspiration. A close look at this large
etching will help one understand how his art differs from
that of other recent figurative artists. The plate contains
two images, one above the other. Below, a man raises his
head upward while directing his gaze toward us. His
form casts a dark shadow on what appears to be the wall
of a cell or dungeon. In places the flesh of his back is torn
open like paper. Above, a male and female lion and a
naked man are linked in an erotic scene from which
emanates a curious tangle composed of lions' tails and a
cord emerging from the man's navel or sexual organ. At
the center there is yet another, even more enigmatic scene
containing a few scribbles and a round object casting a
shadow to the left. What is the meaning of these strange,
mysterious images?

Clemente's title declares that what we see is *Not
St. Girolamo*, not St. Jerome, the church father who
spent part of his life as an ascetic in the wilderness, part
as a scholar translating Hebrew Scriptures into Latin.
The title allows no reference to the canonical
representations of St. Jerome, no revisions of Rogier van
der Weyden's *St. Jerome in the Desert* (1450–64) or of
Dürer's *St. Jerome in his Study* (1514). The title affirms
only its opposite, tempting one to interpret the
composition in precisely the way the artist says is
incorrect. Even though Jerome's traditional symbol is the
lion, usually depicted sleeping at the feet of the studious

saint, the image is dissociated from its traditional
meaning. Hermeneutics in reverse? Iconography without
tradition? The artist's intention may be gleaned from this
provocative statement: "The title is *Not St. Girolamo*,
so that's not St. Jerome. It is . . . just the easiest title to
give a drawing where there is a lion and a man. . . . Keep
to the surface. Don't look for meaning. There is nothing
new in this attitude. In every mystical tradition, whatever
paradoxical or poetic notion you come across, there is
the idea that you don't have to add meaning to it."

The painting *Semen* (1983, no. 46) even more
clearly leaves the viewer on his own, allowing him to
examine his own feelings, make his own associations,
study his own repertory of iconological sources. The
image of a sleeping figure, floating like a fetus in the air
with arms outstretched like angels' wings, evokes no
specific meanings. Painted on raw canvas resembling
handmade paper, *Semen* is rendered with a flatness of
surface typical of a print. The aquatint etching *Not
St. Girolamo* and the colorful, almost expressionist
monotypes (nos. 59–61), on the other hand, present
more painterly versions of print technique than the
medium usually allows. The paradox in Clemente's
approach to technique seems to have a parallel in his
attitude toward meaning and content: St. Girolamo is
not St. Girolamo, and semen gives birth to associations
and notions quite distinct from the traditional
delimitations of iconography.

In a further separation of image from meaning,
Clemente asserts that his self-portrait, which frequently
appears in his paintings, drawings and prints, far from
being "an obsession with self" (the typical, old-fashioned
Freudian interpretation), or a kind of narcissism, as some
observers are quick to assume, is simply another figurative element to be seen as free of presumed meanings.

Like the surrealists, to whose work Clemente's bears
a superficial similiarity, Clemente makes images that
startle the viewer. Unlike the surrealists, who directed
their attention to creating a new vocabulary in order to
elucidate traditional meanings, Clemente produces
images that are not intended to decode meanings. They
are pure inventions with new meanings.

Clemente, also unlike the surrealists, whose concept
presupposed a certain knowledge of iconographical
sources, uses his figurative images for nonnarrative
purposes. In this respect, he also departs from his
contemporaries Sandro Chia, Mimmo Paladino, Anselm
Kiefer and Jörg Immendorff. Clemente's works are
"deconstructive." They do not tell a story, nor do they
provide a description of a situation. Rather, they are
deconstructing reality. Clemente's imagery attempts to
deconstruct the observer's conventional assumption of
what reality is supposed to be. This indeed is the major

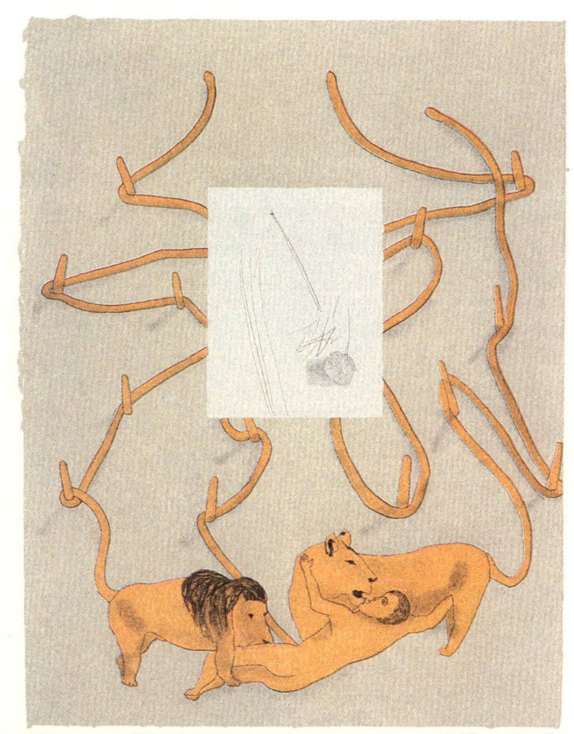

difference between his pictorial inventions and those of many of his contemporaries.

Clemente invents what he calls "unknown ideograms, ideograms in costumes," in which "logic and chance as one force" become effective. It is to that intense experience, hidden in silence, devoid of words, where feeling and thought can be reconciled, that his pictures lead us. And prompt us to ask, as Novalis does: "What is man? A consummate tropism of the mind. Each real intimation is allegory forming—and are endearments real intimations too?"   RC

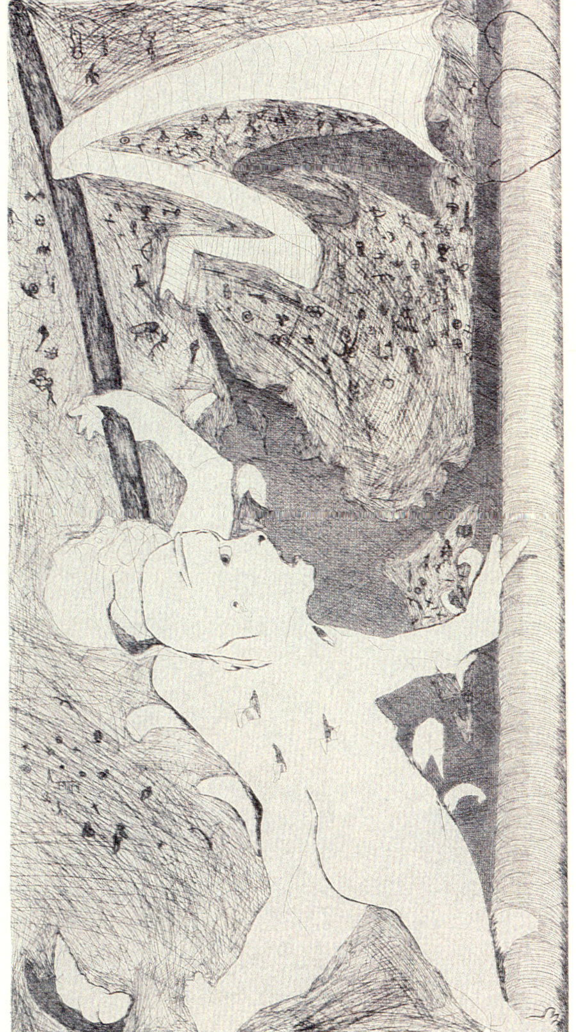

50. *Not St. Girolamo* 1981

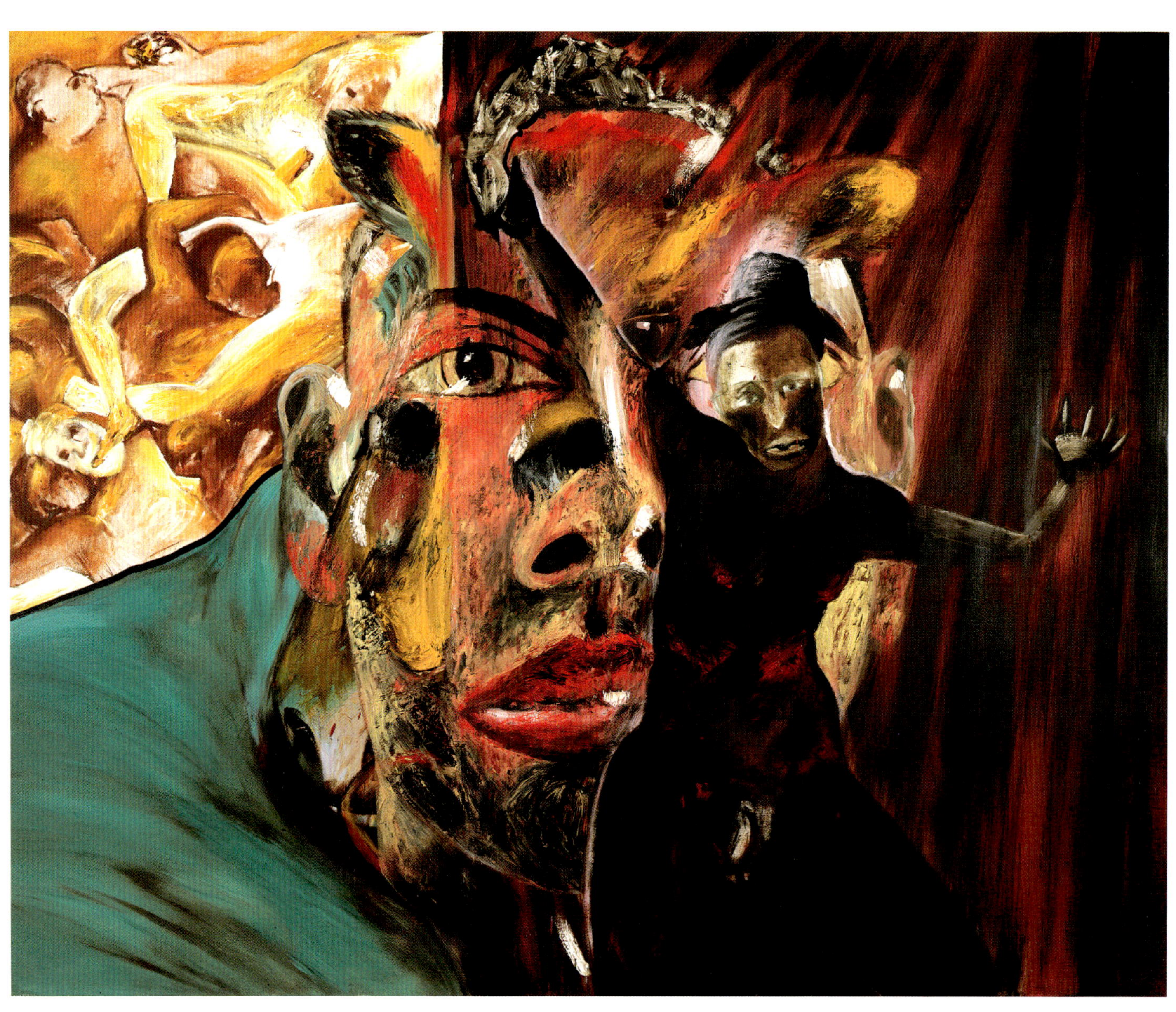

45. Untitled 1983

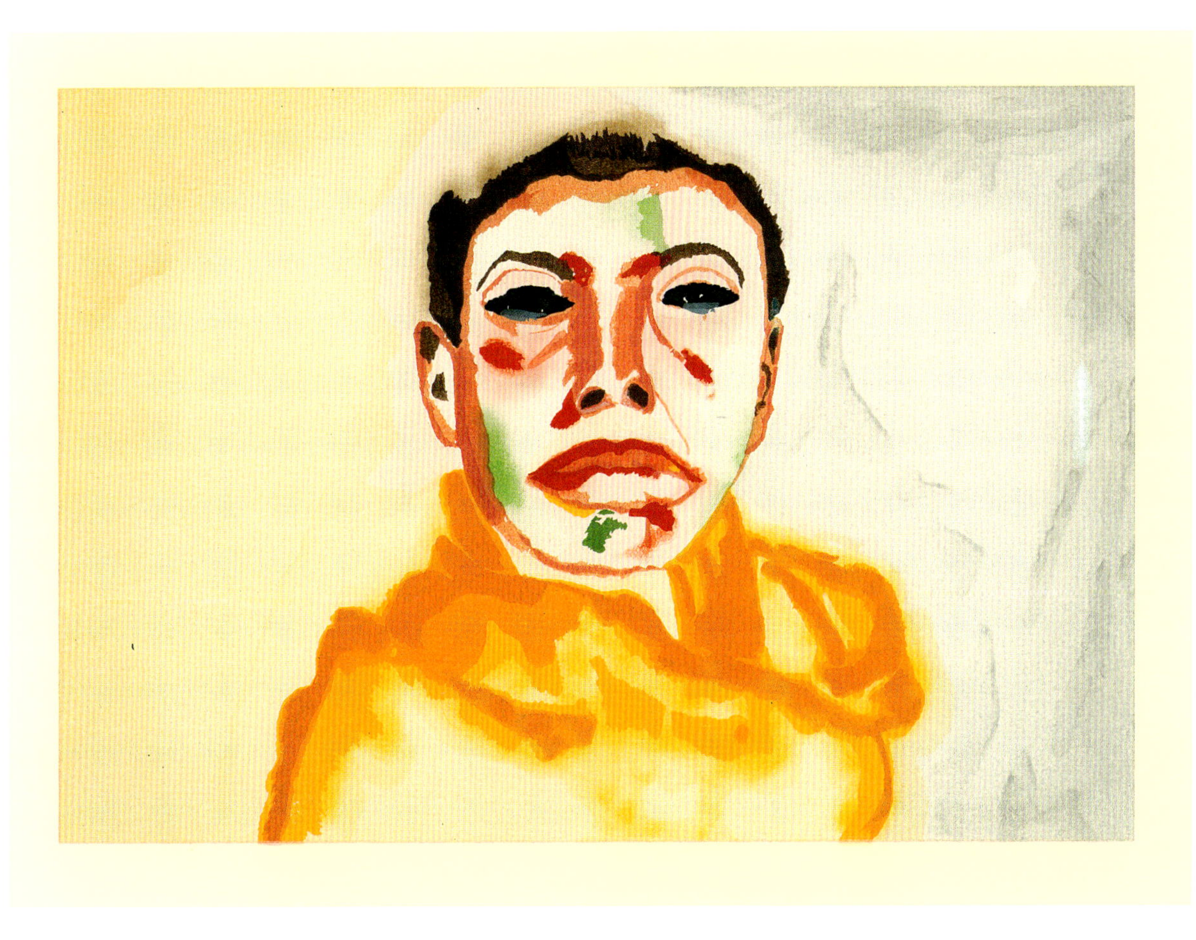

57. I 1982

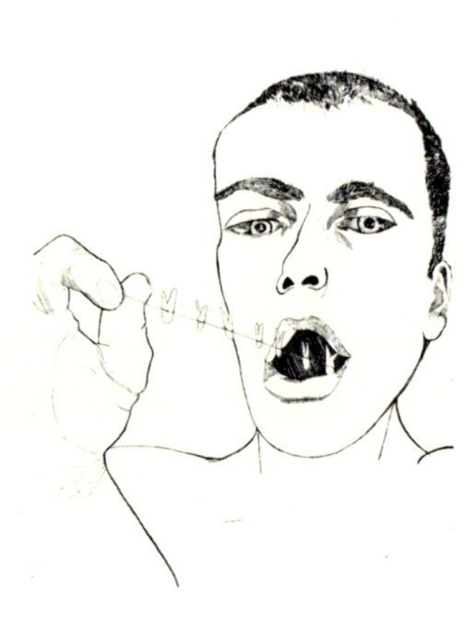

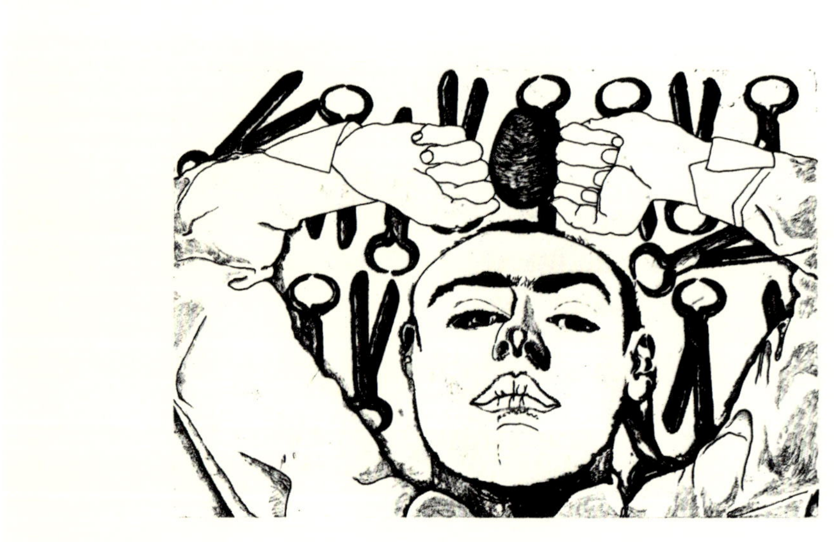

51.   *Self-Portrait #2 (Teeth)*   1981   (top)
52.   *Self-Portrait #3 (Pincers)*   1981

FRANCESCO CLEMENTE

1952
Born in Naples, Italy
Lives in Madras, New York, and Rome

Selected Solo Exhibitions
1975
Gian Enzo Sperone, Rome
Franco Toselli, Milan
1976
Gian Enzo Sperone, Rome
1978
Centre d'art Contemporain, Geneva
Art & Project, Amsterdam
1979
Lisson Gallery, London
Gian Enzo Sperone, Turin
Paul Maenz, Cologne, West Germany
1980
Sperone Westwater Fischer, New York
Padiglione d'Arte Contemporanea di
Milano, Milan (catalogue)
1981
Museum van Hedendaagse Kunst, Ghent,
Belgium
Francesco Clemente/Matrix 46, University
Art Museum, University of California,
Berkeley
Francesco Clemente/Matrix 70, Wadsworth
Atheneum, Hartford, Connecticut
1982
Il Viaggiatore Napoletano, Paul Maenz,
Cologne, West Germany (catalogue)
Francesco Clemente Watercolors, Bruno
Bischofberger, Zürich, Switzerland
(catalogue)
1983
Francesco Clemente: The Fourteen Stations,
Whitechapel Art Gallery, London. Traveled
to Groninger Museum, Groningen, the
Netherlands; Badischer Kunstverein,
Karlsruhe, West Germany (catalogue)
Sperone Westwater and Mary Boone
Gallery, New York
Moderna Museet, Stockholm (catalogue)
Akira Ikeda Gallery, Nagoya and Tokyo,
Japan (catalogue)
1984
Francesco Clemente Pastels, Nationalgalerie
Berlin. Traveled to Museum Folkwang,
Essen, West Germany; Stedelijk Museum,
Amsterdam; Kunsthalle Tübingen,
West Germany (catalogue)
Kunsthalle Basel, Switzerland

Selected Group Exhibitions
1975
XII Bienal, São Paulo, Brazil
1977
Biennale de Paris, Musée d'Art Moderne de
la Ville de Paris
1980
*Die Enthauptete Hand: 100 Zeichnungen
aus Italien*, Bonner Kunstverein, Bonn,
West Germany. Traveled to Städtische
Galerie Wolfsburg; Groninger Museum,
Groningen, the Netherlands (catalogue)
Egonavigatio, Mannheimer Kunstverein,
Mannheim, West Germany (catalogue)
Aperto '80, Venice Biennale

Sieben junge Künstler aus Italien, Kunsthalle
Basel, Switzerland. Traveled to Museum
Folkwang, Essen, West Germany; Stedelijk
Museum, Amsterdam (catalogue)
1981
*Westkunst: Zeitgenössische Kunst seit
1939*, Rheinhallen der Kölner Messe,
Cologne, West Germany (catalogue)
Italians and American Italians, Crown Point
Gallery, Oakland, California (catalogue)
Figures: Forms and Expressions, Albright-
Knox Art Gallery, CEPA Gallery, and
Hallwalls, Buffalo, New York (catalogue)
1982
Documenta 7, Kassel (catalogue)
*New Works on Paper 2: Borofsky,
Clemente, Merz, Penck, Penone*,
The Museum of Modern Art, New York
(catalogue)
Kunst nu/Kunst unserer Zeit, Kunsthalle
Wilhelmshaven, West Germany and
Groninger Museum, Groningen, the
Netherlands (catalogue)
Zeitgeist, Martin Gropius Bau, Berlin
(catalogue)
1983
Chia, Clemente, Cucchi, Kunsthalle
Bielefeld, West Germany. Traveled to
Louisiana Museum, Humlebaek, Denmark
(catalogue)
Expressionist Painting Beyond Picasso,
Basel Art Fair, Switzerland
Recent European Painting, The Solomon R.
Guggenheim Museum, New York
(catalogue)
1984
The Folding Image, National Gallery of Art,
Washington, D.C. (catalogue)
*An International Survey of Recent Painting
and Sculpture*, The Museum of Modern Art,
New York (catalogue)

CHECKLIST

Paintings
45.   Untitled   1983
oil on canvas
78 x 93 (198.1 x 236.2)
Collection Gerald S. Elliott, Chicago
46.   *Semen*   1983
oil on canvas
93 x 156 (236.2 x 396.2)
Collection Mrs. Gustavo Cisneros, Caracas,
Venezuela

Sculptures
47.   *Analogy*   1983
fresco on radiator
34 x 17 x 3¼ (86.4 x 43.2 x 8.3)
Courtesy Sperone Westwater, New York
48.   *Breathe*   1983
fresco on concrete block fragment
13½ x 16 x 5½ (34.3 x 40.6 x 14)
Courtesy Sperone Westwater, New York
49.   *Saint*   1983
fresco on metal beam with chain
4 x 34 x 4 (10.2 x 86.4 x 10.2)
Courtesy Sperone Westwater, New York

Prints
50.   *Not St. Girolamo*   1981
etching, drypoint on paper; edition: 25
image: 61 x 19 (154.9 x 48.3)
sheet: 63 x 24½ (160 x 62.2)
Courtesy Crown Point Press, Oakland,
Calif. and New York
51.   *Self-Portrait #2 (Teeth)*   1981
etching on paper; edition: 10
image: 6 x 8 (15.2 x 20.3)
sheet: 16 x 20½ (40.6 x 52)
Courtesy Crown Point Press, Oakland,
Calif. and New York
52.   *Self-Portrait #3 (Pincers)*   1981
etching on paper; edition: 10
image: 13⅛ x 19⅛ (33.3 x 48.6)
sheet: 16 x 20½ (40.6 x 52)
Courtesy Crown Point Press, Oakland,
Calif. and New York
53.   *Self-Portrait #6 (Stoplight)*   1981
etching on paper; edition: 10
image: 13⅛ x 19⅛ (33.3 x 48.6)
sheet: 16 x 20½ (40.6 x 52)
Courtesy Crown Point Press, Oakland,
Calif. and New York
54.   *Telemone #1*   1981
etching on paper; edition: 25
image: 61 x 19 (154.9 x 48.3)
sheet: 63 x 24½ (160 x 62.2)
Courtesy Crown Point Press, Oakland,
Calif. and New York
55.   *Telemone #2*   1981
etching on paper; edition: 25
image: 61 x 19 (154.9 x 40.3)
sheet: 63 x 26 (160 x 66)
Courtesy Crown Point Press, Oakland,
Calif. and New York
56.   *This Side Up*   1981
woodcut on paper; edition: 25
image: 19 x 39¼ (48.3 x 99.7)
sheet: 29 x 48¾ (73.7 x 123.8)
Courtesy Crown Point Press, Oakland,
Calif. and New York
57.   *I*   1982
woodcut on paper; edition: 100
image: 14⅛ x 20⅛ (35.9 x 51.1)
sheet: 16⅞ x 22½ (42.9 x 57.2)
Collection Walker Art Center, Minneapolis
58.   *Morning*   1982
woodcut on paper; edition: 100
image: 19 x 61 (48.3 x 154.9)
sheet: 24 x 63 (61 x 160)
Courtesy Crown Point Press, Oakland,
Calif. and New York
59.   Untitled   1983
monotype on paper
image: 20 x 14 (50.8 x 35.6)
sheet: 42 x 29½ (106.7 x 74.9)
Courtesy Petersburg Press, New York
60.   Untitled   1983
monotype on paper
image: 40 x 30 (101.6 x 76.2)
sheet: 48 x 39 (121.9 x 99.1)
Courtesy Petersburg Press, New York
61.   Untitled   1983
monotype on paper
image: 20 x 17 (50.8 x 43.2)
sheet: 42 x 29 (106.7 x 73.7)
Courtesy Petersburg Press, New York

ROGER HERMAN

Roger Herman frequently borrows both stylistic elements and subject matter from the art of the past, using them in making his large, thickly painted canvases and rough-hewn woodcuts. Although images from art history such as Vincent van Gogh's troubled self-portraits and Jean François Millet's poignant realist paintings of peasants are Herman's primary source material, he also relies on other familiar imagery from popular culture, to photographs of his parents, to representations of mythical knights and dragons. In a manner both mocking and serious Herman questions the myth of total commitment and sacrifice to art perpetuated by history in speaking of such predecessors as van Gogh, Millet and even Jackson Pollock. For him, the history of art is an endless source of images and techniques to be combined to completely new effect.

Born in Saarbrücken, West Germany, in 1947, Herman studied philosophy and law before beginning to paint in 1972. His early work was socially and conceptually oriented. He worked in several media, including painting, photography and film. In 1976, following his graduation from the Kunstakademie in Karlsruhe, he came to the United States. His attraction to the figurative work of Bay Area artists led him to San Francisco, but his growing camaraderie with a group of Los Angeles artists prompted him to move there in 1981.

Herman spends much of his time making woodcuts, a medium to which he was drawn after seeing a large Jim Dine woodcut in the works in 1981. He follows no prescription for making paintings and prints of the same subject; if he likes an image in one medium, he often tries it in another. His painting *Van Gogh* (1983, no. 62) and woodcut *Van Gogh in Red* (1983, no. 66) are overtly romanticized pictures of the saintly artist tormented by his own genius. Both are large in scale, reinforcing van Gogh's stature as a tragic hero. The painting consists of several layers of pigment, seemingly applied with housepainter's brushes, resulting in an image of great physical weight. This quality is echoed in the woodcut, created from two coarsely chiseled eight-by-four-foot plywood panels. Both the gestural brushwork and raw woodcuts ally Herman with his German Expressionist ancestors. However, none of the *angst* associated with German Expressionism can be found in Herman's work. Instead, his oversized images are more nearly caricatures of the art on which they are based.

Herman often paints from slides projected onto the canvas. In this manner, he concentrates on process rather than on the specific image. While the blues, greens and purples in the painting *Van Gogh* lend it a cool, distant quality, the fiery orange and red colors of the woodcut transform it into a striking and powerful image. The figure in the woodcut is simple and heavily outlined in black, set in contrast by brilliant turgid gashes. For Herman, making a woodcut is like making a large draw-

ing; the difficulty of the process forces him to be more precise than he is in his works based on slides. The simple posterlike quality of the woodcut *Van Gogh*, emphasized by its monochromatic hues, renders it a more elemental icon than the heavily encrusted painted version.

In using van Gogh's *Self-Portrait* (1888) and Millet's field workers (see *Fieldwork,* 1984, no. 68) as his own, Herman has, like the Pop artists of the late 1950s and early 60s, taken a private icon and turned it into a heroic emblem. His transformation of van Gogh's *Self-Portrait* into a monumental and somewhat garish image demystifies the previous work. It signals the distancing of a "sacred" art historical image. "Van Gogh was the first cliché of Expressionism," Herman remarks. "I think our image of him as the selfless painter was partially fostered by art history. We like to stylize people into this tragic role. Yet I'm interested in what he stood for, in his commitment to making serious art. . . . I still long for the traditional position of an artist, but it doesn't seem like a very realistic role to play today." Ultimately, there is a dichotomy in Herman's attitude toward the art of the past; respectful of the work of van Gogh, for instance, he questions history's overemphasis on the famous Dutch master's tragic story rather than on his art.

Herman painted *Vater, Mutter, Heidelberg* (1983, no. 63) and made the three woodcuts in *Fatherland, Mothertongue* (1983, no. 65) after staged photographs of his parents, who commissioned the pictures in the 1940s. Herman creates a contrast between his subjective, sentimental feelings for his mother and father and the glossy, idealized images they themselves commissioned for posterity. "When I made the woodcut of my parents I wanted to make it look like a poster rather than a more personal image. . . . I wanted it to have a heroic quality, despite the fact that they are just my parents. They look like movie stars." The addition of the knight and the dragon to *Fatherland, Mothertongue* lends the triptych a fairytale quality. It suggests an attempt on the artist's part to be reserved and cool, showing an ambivalence toward the subject. Herman sees this inability to present poignant images realistically as a characteristic of his generation.

Herman claims that printmaking has improved his ability to draw. Interviewed in 1983 for the catalogue of an exhibition at the University of Redlands, California, Herman noted: "The woodcuts are ahead of my paintings, because I'm really naive about them. . . . With a painting, I'm aware of so much history–I'm wondering whether it should be done loose or firm, fast or slow. Doing the woodcuts has kept my paintings cleaner. . . . What I like about the woodcuts . . . is that the roughness [puts them] at a remove–it gives them a distance and austerity. They look modern . . . but they also look like Gothic church art."   FI

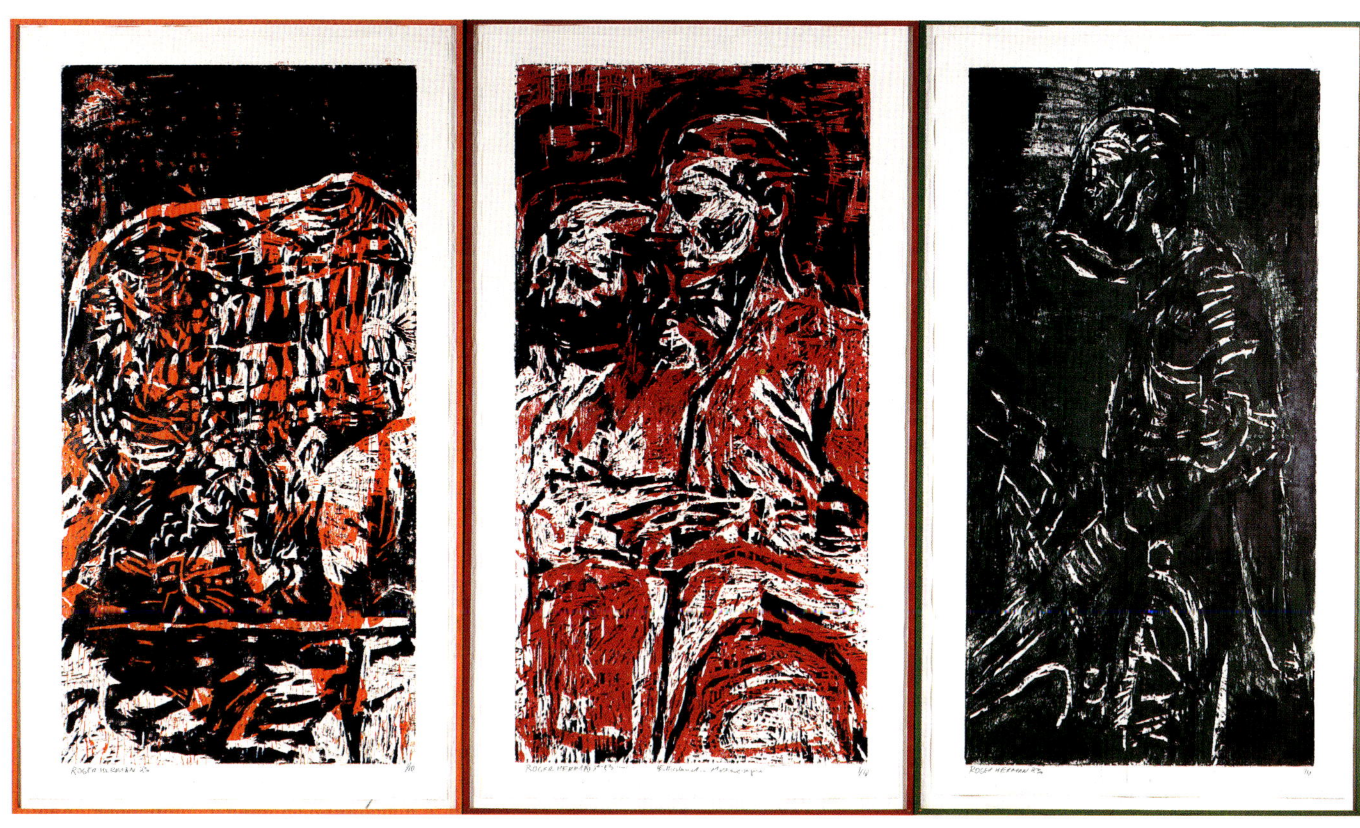

65. *Fatherland, Mothertongue*   1983

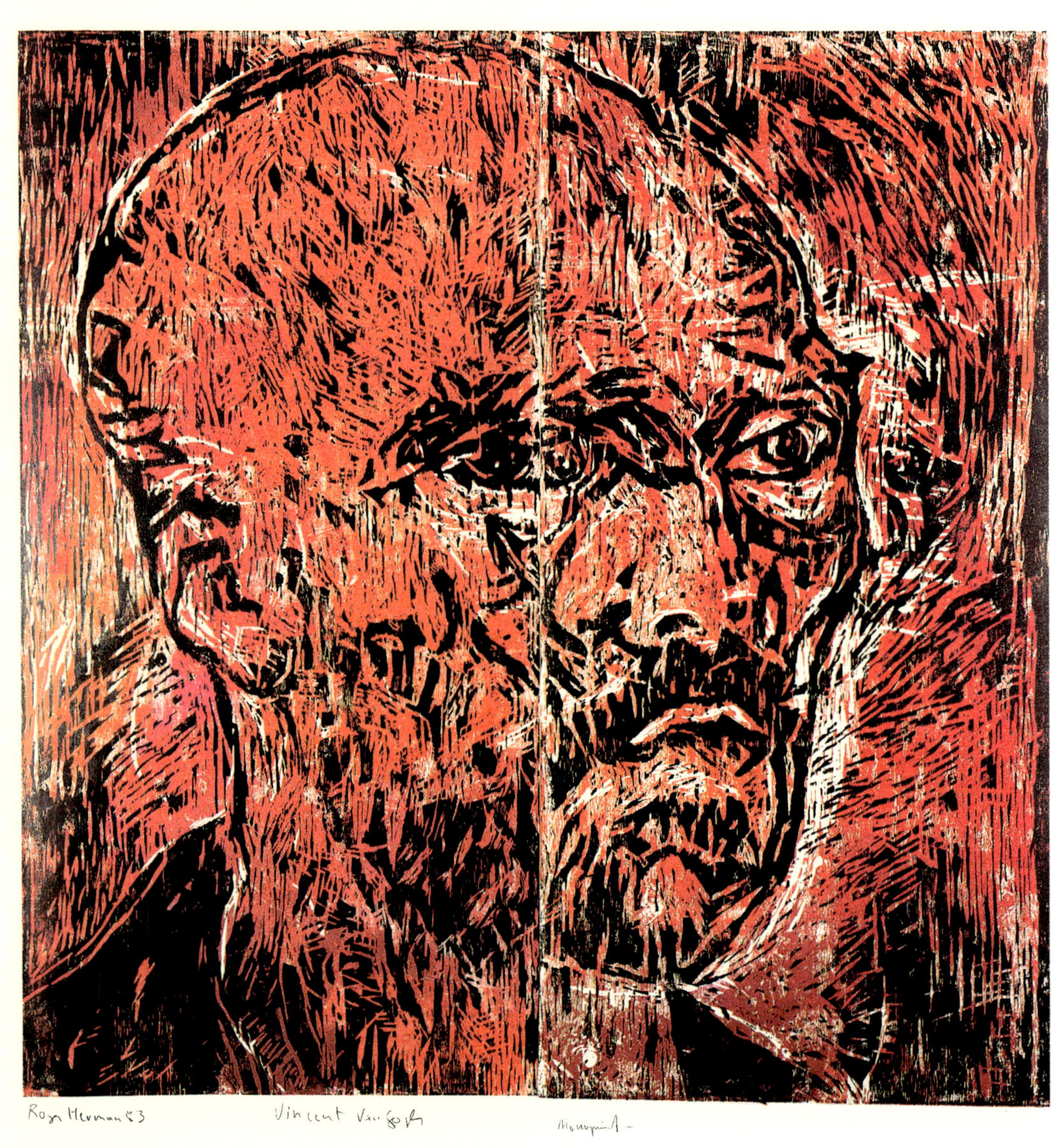

66. *Van Gogh in Red* 1983

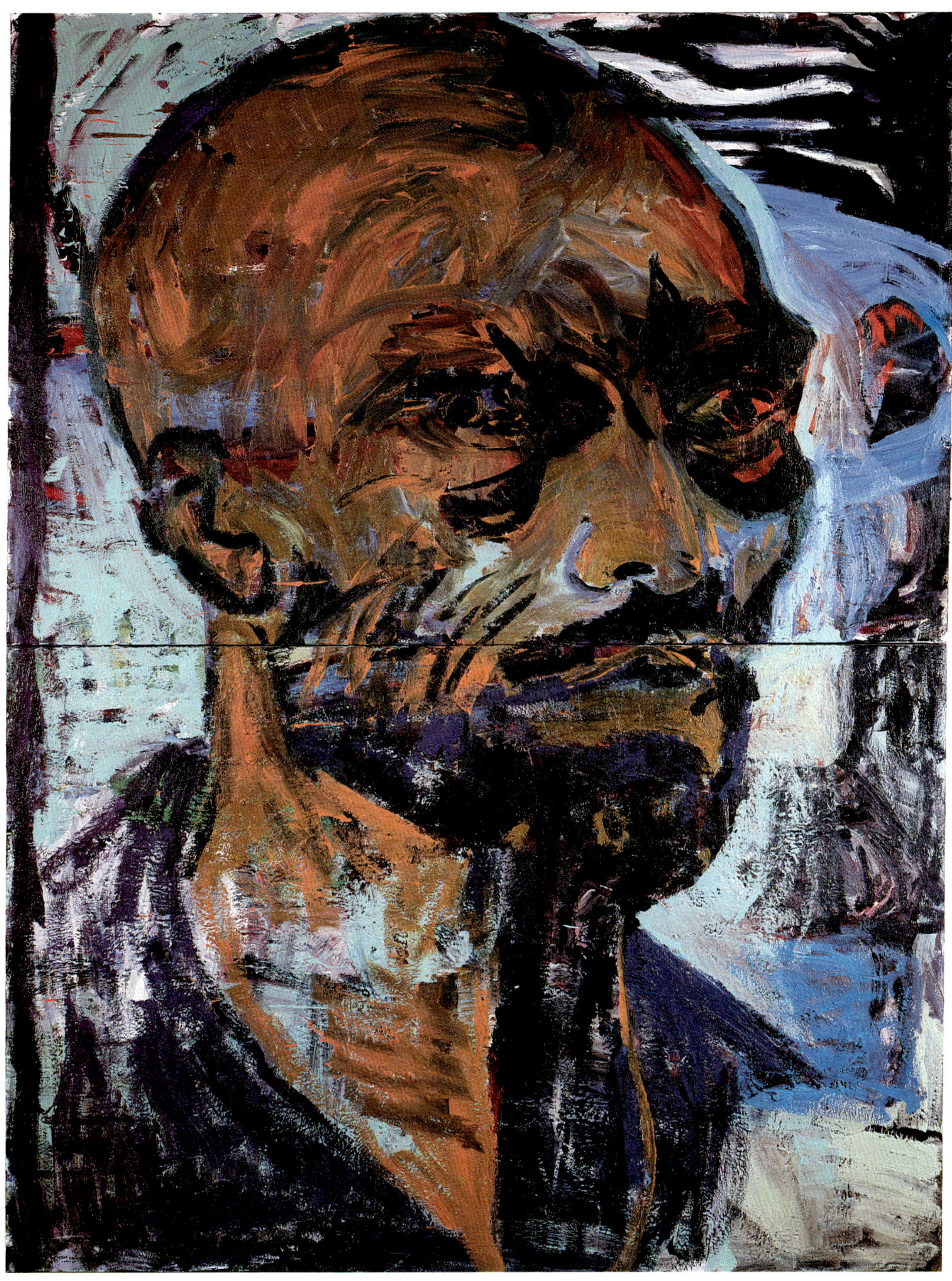

62. *Van Gogh* 1983

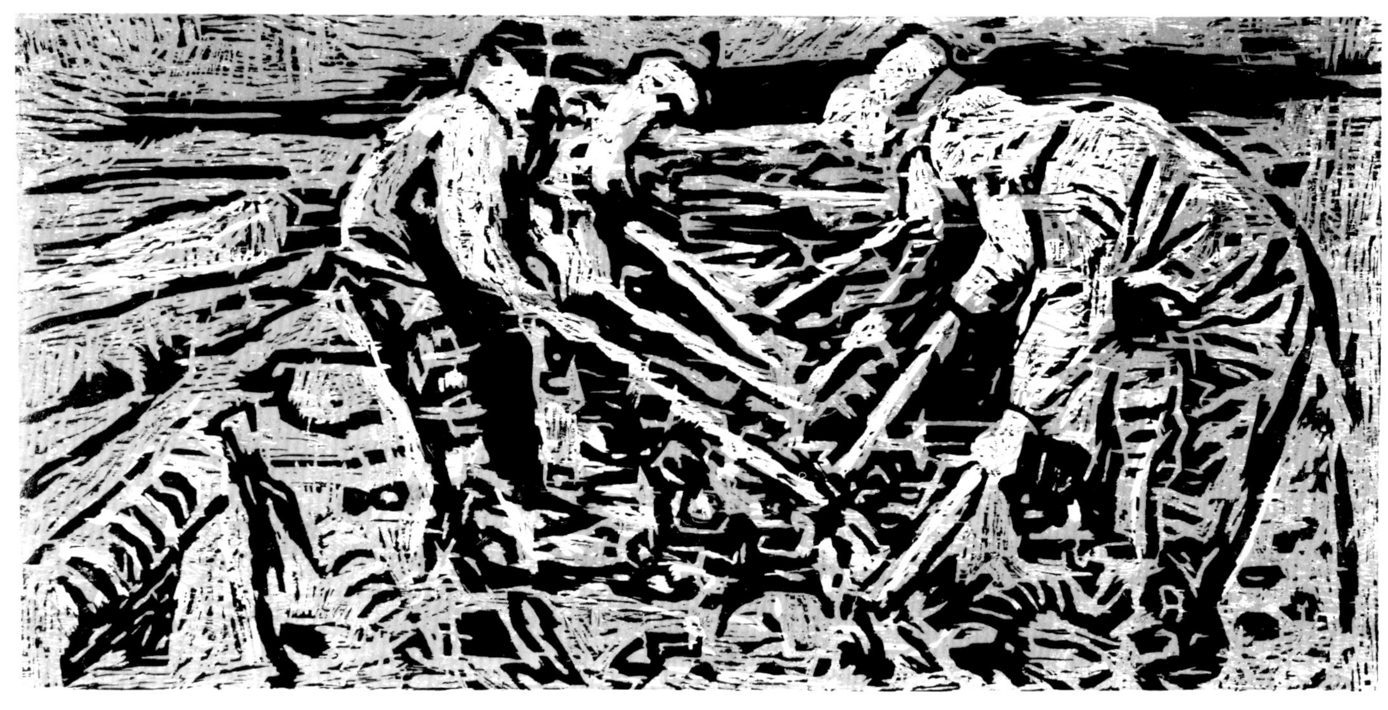

68. *Fieldwork* 1984

ROGER HERMAN

1947
Born in Saarbrücken, Saarland,
West Germany
1972 – 76
Attended the Kunstakademie, Karlsruhe,
West Germany
Lives in Los Angeles

Solo Exhibitions
1973
Galerie am Neumarkt, Saarbrücken,
West Germany
1977
Goethe Institute, San Francisco
1979
Dana Reich Gallery, San Francisco
(catalogue)
1980
Jetwave, San Francisco
1981
San Francisco Art Institute
Ulrike Kantor Gallery, Los Angeles
Beyond Good and Evil, Southern Exposure,
San Francisco
1982
Kunstakademie, Karlsruhe, West Germany
(catalogue)
Ulrike Kantor Gallery, Los Angeles
1983
Eaton/Shoen Gallery, San Francisco
Ulrike Kantor Gallery, Los Angeles
(catalogue)
La Jolla Museum of Contemporary Art,
California (brochure)
Peppers Art Gallery, University of Redlands,
California (catalogue)
1984
Hal Bromm Gallery, New York
Roger Ramsey, Chicago
Eaton/Shoen Gallery, San Francisco
Ulrike Kantor Gallery, Los Angeles
Patti Aande, San Diego

Selected Group Exhibitions
1976
Badischer Kunstverein, Karlsruhe,
West Germany
1979
Gestures (with John Ford), Center for the
Visual Arts, Oakland, California
1981
New Fauve Painting: A Selected Exhibition,
California State University, Los Angeles
(catalogue)
Figuration, University Art Museum,
University of California, Santa Barbara
(catalogue)
Fresh Paint, San Francisco Museum of
Modern Art
Four LA Painters, Pasadena City College
Gallery, California
Critics Choice, Eaton/Shoen Gallery,
San Francisco
New Painting and Sculpture, San Francisco
Art Institute (catalogue)

1983
Palm Springs Desert Museum, California
(catalogue)
Ten by Ten, Los Angeles Institute of
Contemporary Art
1984
The Human Condition: Biennial III,
San Francisco Museum of Modern Art
(catalogue)
Portraits, The Institute for Art and Urban
Resources, P.S. 1, Long Island City,
New York

CHECKLIST

Paintings
62. *Van Gogh* 1983
oil on canvas
132 x 98 (335.3 x 248.9)
Courtesy Ulrike Kantor Gallery,
Los Angeles
63. *Vater, Mutter, Heidelberg
(Father, Mother, Heidelberg)* 1983
oil on canvas
48 x 51 (121.9 x 129.5)
Courtesy Ulrike Kantor Gallery,
Los Angeles

Prints
64. *Self-Portrait with Palette* 1982
woodcut on linen; edition: 10
image: 48 x 48 (121.9 x 121.9)
sheet: 72 x 60 (182.9 x 152.4)
Courtesy Ulrike Kantor Gallery,
Los Angeles
65. *Fatherland, Mothertongue* 1983
three woodcuts on paper; edition: 10
image: 96 x 48 each (243.8 x 121.9)
sheet: 108 x 60 each (274.3 x 152.4)
Courtesy Ulrike Kantor Gallery,
Los Angeles
66. *Van Gogh in Red* 1983
woodcut on paper; edition: 3
image: 96 x 96 (243.8 x 243.8)
sheet: 120 x 108 (304.8 x 274.3)
Courtesy Ulrike Kantor Gallery,
Los Angeles
67. *Woman Carrying Bananas* 1983
woodcut on paper; edition: 10
image: 96 x 48 (243.3 x 121.9)
sheet: 108 x 60 (274.3 x 152.4)
Courtesy Ulrike Kantor Gallery,
Los Angeles
68. *Fieldwork* 1984
woodcut on paper; edition: 10
image: 48 x 96 (121.9 x 243.3)
sheet: 60 x 108 (152.4 x 274.3)
Courtesy Ulrike Kantor Gallery,
Los Angeles

JÖRG IMMENDORFF

'Thinking' now seems to me a sort of 'behavior,' an attitude, a taking a stand. The whole body takes part in it with all the senses.
Bertolt Brecht, *Messingkauf Dialogues*

On first seeing the paintings and prints of Jörg Immendorff, one can immediately draw stylistic comparisons to European and American artists of the 1920s and 30s: the German New Objectivity painters George Grosz and Otto Dix; the American social realists Jack Levine, Reginald Marsh and Ben Shahn; and even the Mexican muralists José Clemente Orozco, Diego Rivera and David Alfaro Siqueiros. Yet this is not an adequate reading of Immendorff's art. Despite its seemingly harmless narrative, its calculated naivete and apparent propaganda, there is, in Immendorff's work, concern with image-making and storytelling that is overpowering. Our attention is in fact held by the artist's Brechtian cynicism toward the current state of world affairs.

One of today's foremost East German writers and poets, Heiner Müller, declared in 1982: "I wish to stand with one leg on either side of the [Berlin] wall. That might be a schizophrenic position, but no other seems more real to me. I believe in conflict. Otherwise, I don't believe in anything. Answers and solutions–they don't interest me." This statement accurately reflects Immendorff's feelings and his position within contemporary painting. Disinterested in questions of form, style and conceptual novelty, he is dedicated to the pursuit of "painting with moral substance." He sees his art as "a contribution to the sum of cultural production, jointly created by my colleagues and me in a loosely woven fabric of positions and counterpositions."

Born in 1945 in northern Germany, in a town located on the west side of the Elbe, the river dividing West from East Germany, Jörg Immendorff took part in the 1968 student demonstrations and anti-Vietnam activities in West Germany, where his art and his philosophical position were formed. Since his student days at the Kunstakademie Düsseldorf, where he was involved in the neo-Dada happenings of the Fluxus group, Immendorff has been a disciple of Joseph Beuys and has often publicly associated himself with this man who has dominated the German art scene since the mid-1960s. Much of Immendorff's work from that time, for example, *Beuysland* (1965), relates in concept as well as style to that of Beuys. Immendorff describes himself as a "politically engaged painter; ideological and political determination run like a red thread through my art and my life." In 1983, on the occasion of his major retrospective at the Kunsthaus Zurich, he reaffirmed this position, declaring that "even today, art is the only way for me to clarify and to manifest my political viewpoint."

Immendorff's statement is substantiated by his series of paintings, begun in 1978, entitled *Café Deutschland*. The mad, apocalyptic bar-cafe of this series represents the artist's attempt to unite the divided world of the two Germanys. "I offer my world," Immendorff says of Café Deutschland, "which is constructed from and nurtured by real experience and authentic visual information." The series originated in his meeting with East German painter Ralf Winkler, better known as A. R. Penck, in 1976. There ensued a series of real and imaginary encounters with Penck to dramatize the separation of the two countries. In Café Deutschland, spies, informers and secret policemen in trenchcoats mingle with political leaders of the two governments and with Immendorff and Penck themselves. Figuring in several of the paintings is the eagle, symbolizing the West German state; the watchtowers enable the leaders of both countries to spy on their people.

Although the seemingly chaotic formal arrangement and composition of Immendorff's paintings might cause one to dismiss them, their inner movement is compelling. This magnetism is intensified in his large-scale linoleum-block prints, which are made on the scale of his paintings. In working with linocut, Immendorff endorses one of the most primitive print media. The reduction of line and surface and the relatively unsophisticated technical implications of the process are responsible for the near disappearance of this technique among professional artists. Long popular only in the craft workshop, this simple print form attracted Immendorff for its almost instant identification with the man in the street. In some instances, he transfers imagery from a painting to a linocut, as with *Café Deutschland XII/Adlerhälfte* (1982), from which he made five-by-seven-foot reworkings in linocut (nos. 77–80); in the final print, of course, the image is reversed.

Familiar images appear in these linocuts, including the nearly broken half eagle (*Adlërhalfte*), symbolizing a "crippled" West German state; the artist himself with his head pushed through a poster of Mao; a model of the Brandenburg Gate dividing East and West Berlin, surveyed by heads of Marx, Stalin and Lenin.

Immendorff attempts to go beyond a simple imitative rendering of reality. "Simple, well-known signs create the first contact with the audience," he says. "The second step, which opens up a meeting of the minds, is directed toward the instincts. My art is not fashionable. It is necessary art in terms of politics–accomplished through its figurative imagery and its painterly technique."   RC

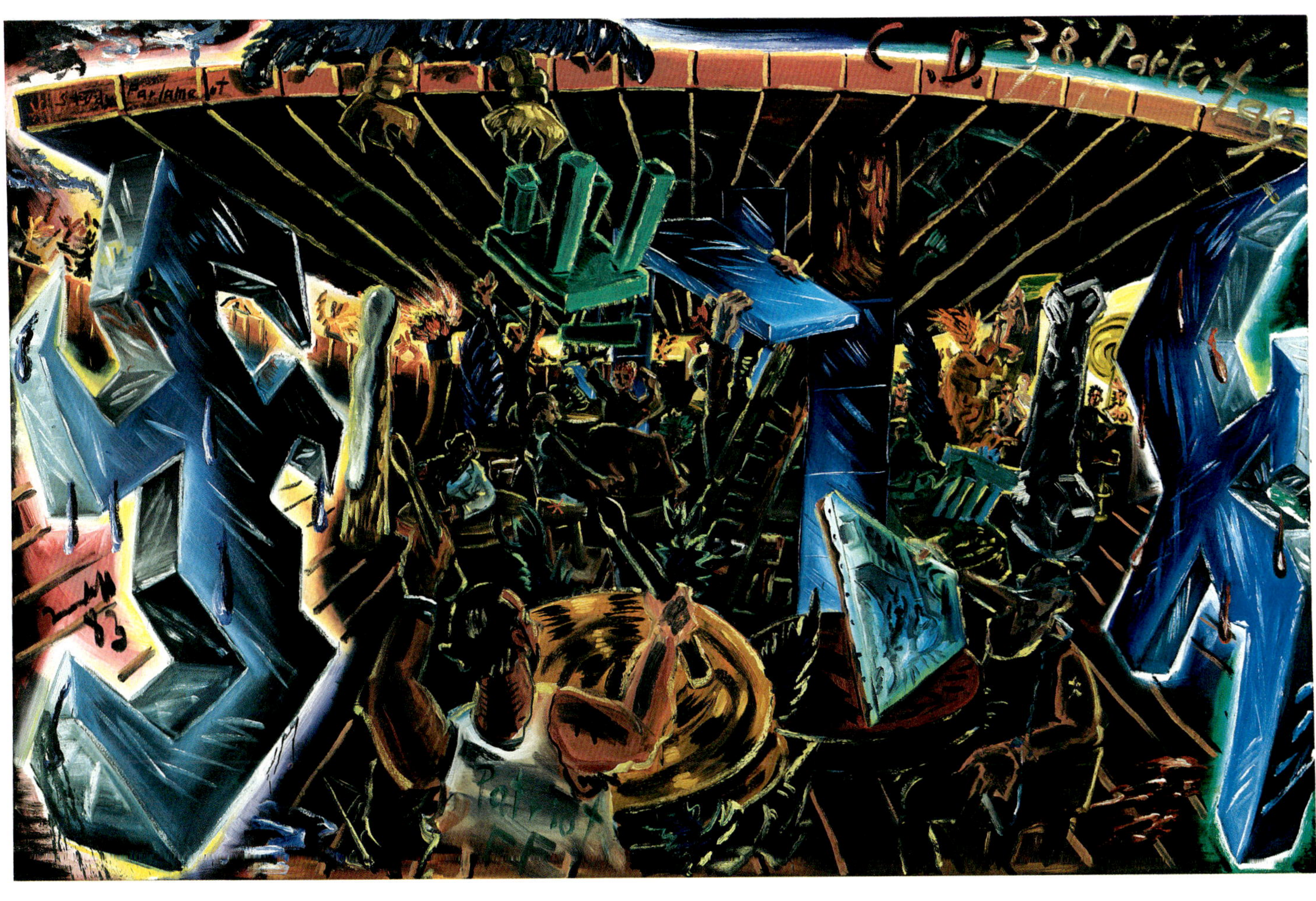

69.   *Café Deutschland 38. Parteitag*   1983

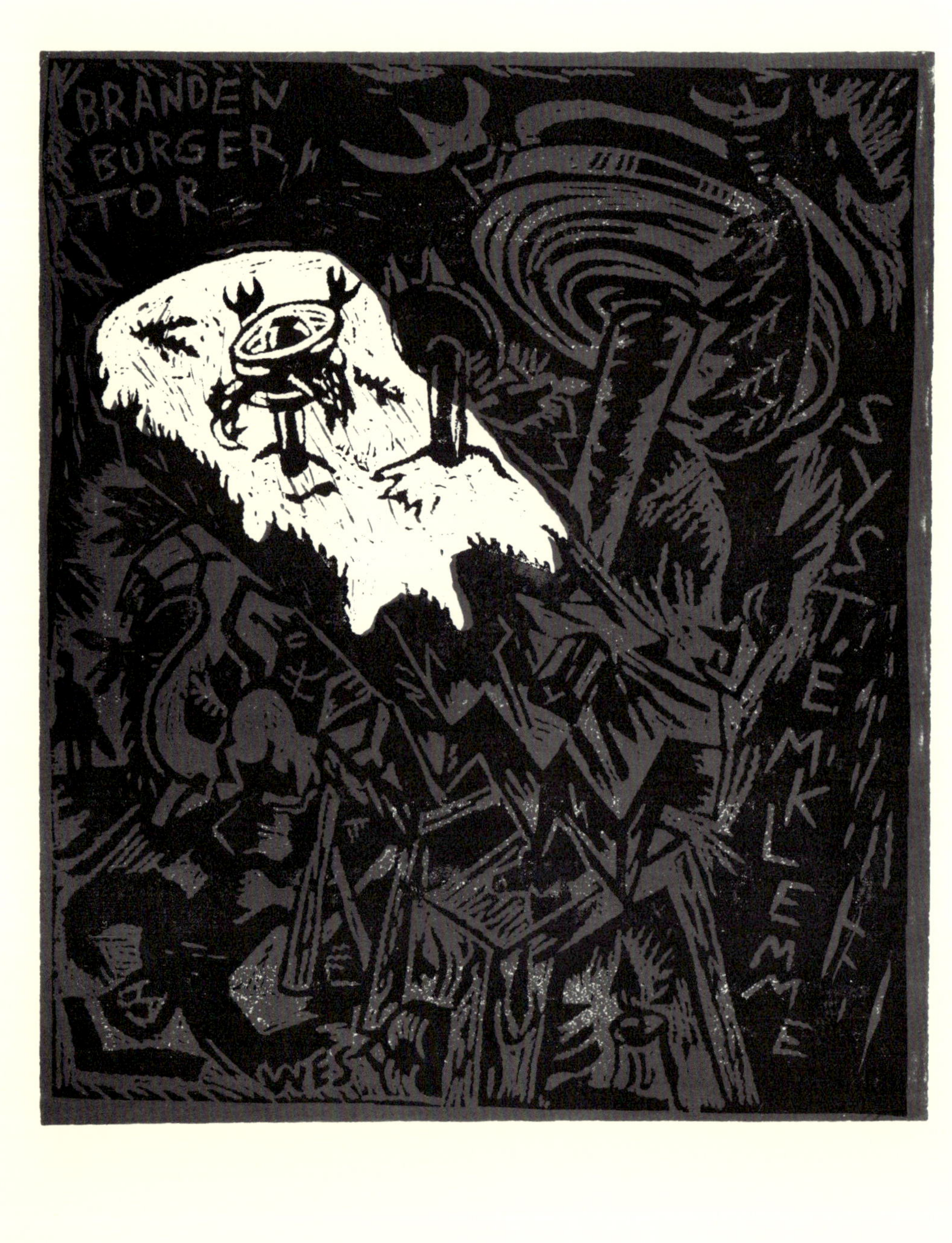

71. *Brandenburger Tor* 1982

72. *Ausgangspunkt* 1982

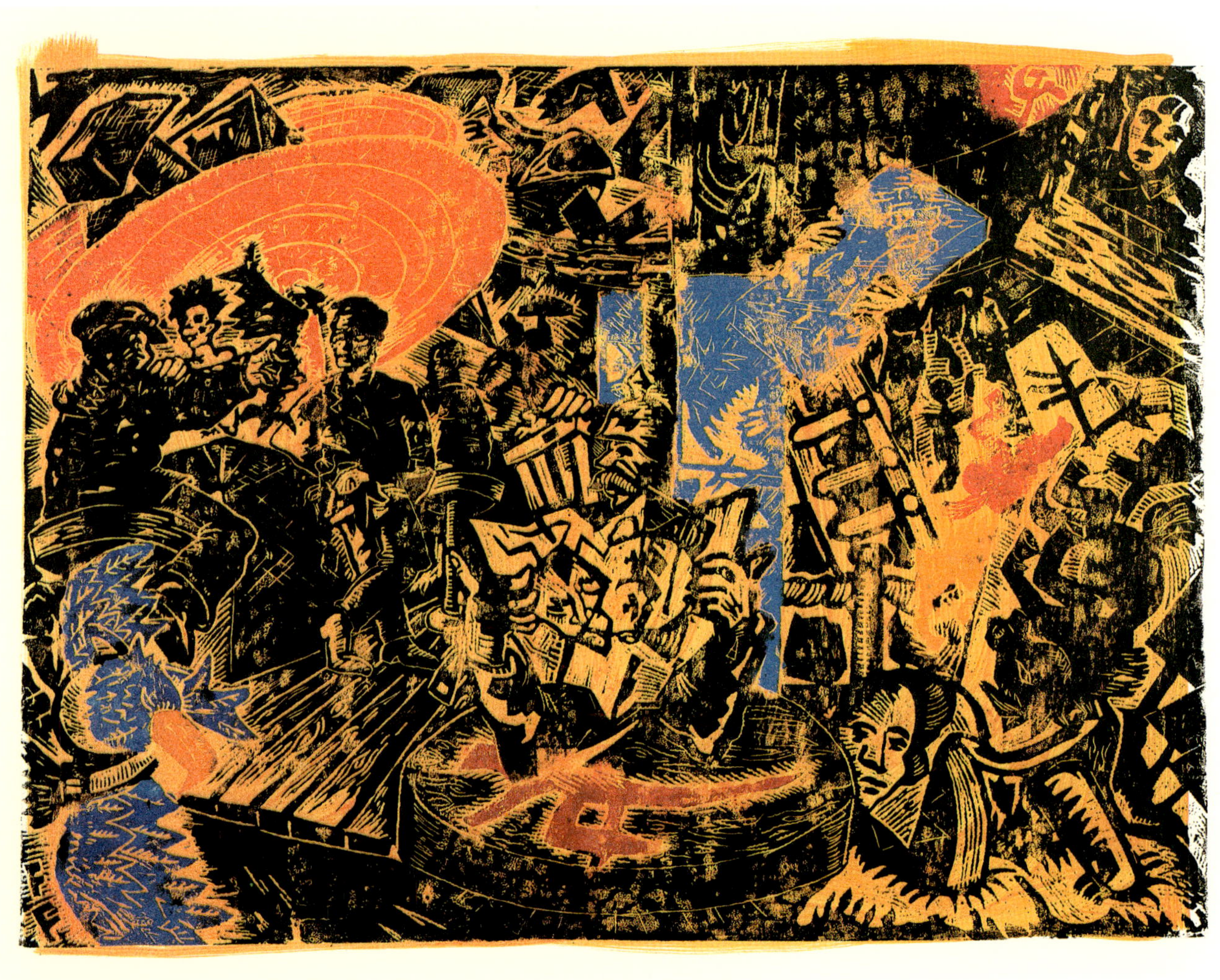

78. *Wir Kommen* 1982

JÖRG IMMENDORFF

1945
Born in Bleckede, Germany
1963–65
Attended the Kunstakademie, Düsseldorf,
West Germany
Lives in Düsseldorf

Selected Solo Exhibitions
1965
Galerie Schmela, Düsseldorf,
West Germany
1969
Galerie Michael Werner, Cologne,
West Germany
1971
Galerie Michael Werner, Cologne,
West Germany
Galerie Heiner Friedrich, Munich,
West Germany
1972
Galerie Michael Werner, Cologne,
West Germany
1973
Hier und jetzt: Das tun was zu tun ist,
Westfälischer Kunstverein, Münster,
West Germany
1976
Galerie Seriaal/Helen van der Meij,
Amsterdam
1979
Café Deutschland, Kunstmuseum Basel,
Switzerland
Teilbau (a permanent open-air exhibition),
Bleckede an der Elbe, West Germany
1980
Malermut rundum, Kunsthalle Bern,
Switzerland
1981
Pinselwiderstand (4X), Stedelijk Van
Abbemuseum, Eindhoven, the Netherlands
1982
Café Deutschland/Adlerhälfte, Kunsthalle
Düsseldorf, West Germany
Sonnabend Gallery, New York
1983
Stedelijk Van Abbemuseum, Eindhoven,
the Netherlands
Kunsthalle Düsseldorf, West Germany
Sonnabend Gallery, New York
Kunsthaus Zürich, Switzerland
1984
Mary Boone Gallery, New York

Selected Group Exhibitions
1969
Düsseldorfer Szene, Kunstmuseum Luzern,
Lucerne, Switzerland
1970
Jetzt, Kunsthalle, Cologne, West Germany
1972
Documenta 5, Kassel, West Germany
(catalogue)
Zeichnungen 2, Städtisches Museum/
Schloss Morsbroich, Leverkusen,
West Germany

1973
Bilder/Objekte/Filme/Konzept, Städtische
Galerie im Lenbachhaus, Munich,
West Germany
1974
XX Internationales Kunstgespräch,
Galerie Nächst St. Stephan, Vienna
1976
Venice Biennale
1977
*Zeitgenössische Kunst aus der Sammlung
des Stedelijk Van Abbemuseum Eindhoven*,
Kunsthalle Bern, Switzerland
1979
Solidaritätsaktion für Jochen Hiltmann,
Stedelijk Van Abbemuseum, Eindhoven,
the Netherlands
Malerei auf Papier, Badischer Kunstverein,
Karlsruhe, West Germany
1980
Venice Biennale
1981
Art d'Allemagne d'Aujourd'hui, Musée
d'Art Moderne de la Ville de Paris
Der Hund stösst im Laufe der Woche zu mir,
Moderna Museet, Stockholm
*Westkunst: Zeitgenössische Kunst seit
1939*, Rheinhallen der Kölner Messe,
Cologne, West Germany (catalogue)
1982
German Drawings of the 60's, Yale
University Art Gallery, New Haven,
Connecticut
4th Biennale of Sydney: Vision in Disbelief,
Sydney, Australia
Documenta 7, Kassel, West Germany
(catalogue)
*Vergangenheit, Gegenwart, Zukunft:
Zeitgenössische Kunst und Architektur*,
Württembergischer Kunstverein, Stuttgart,
West Germany
Zeitgeist, Martin Gropius Bau, Berlin
(catalogue)
1983
*New Figuration. Contemporary Art from
Germany*, Frederick S. Wight Art Gallery,
University of California, Los Angeles
New Painting from Germany,
Tel Aviv Museum, Israel
New Art, The Tate Gallery, London
(catalogue)
Expressions: New Art from Germany,
The Saint Louis Art Museum. Traveled to
The Institute for Art and Urban Resources,
P.S. 1, Long Island City, New York;
Institute of Contemporary Art, University
of Pennsylvania, Philadelphia; The
Contemporary Arts Center, Cincinnati;
Museum of Contemporary Art, Chicago;
Newport Harbor Art Museum, Newport
Beach, California; Corcoran Gallery of Art,
Washington, D.C. (catalogue)
1984
*An International Survey of Recent Painting
and Sculpture*, The Museum of Modern Art,
New York (catalogue)

MIMMO PALADINO

Mimmo Paladino's art, steeped in the long history of Italian culture, reflects a variety of styles and sensibilities, both ancient and modern. Yet, for all their historicism, his painting, sculpture and prints appear to spring as much from the imagination as from any other source. His work is quietly religious and disturbingly demonic. His forms are macabre, dreamlike and surreal, and often focus on death.

Born in Paduli, near Naples, in 1948, Paladino now lives in Milan, and though he has shown his work in Italy since 1976, he did not have his first U.S. exhibition until 1980. He is one of a growing number of young European artists who have refocused attention on expressionist imagery. His prints range from *Gocce nella Valle* of 1982 (no. 87), filled with swirling forms, to the simple and delicate etching *Con Musica* (1980, no. 85) and the small, colorful, iconic wood engravings in his precious book *Bosforo* (1983, no. 91). He often combines several printmaking methods in one image, so that some of his prints are virtual glossaries of techniques. He claims that the character of an image is defined by the medium he uses. "I am totally incapable of attaching myself to a specific technique," he explains. "I rely much more on the discovery of the moment, of happenstance." Thus his wood engravings recall medieval illuminated manuscripts, while his etchings evoke the flowing, visionary images of Edvard Munch's distorted figures and dreamy landscapes.

The tone of the four etchings in the 1983 portfolio *Tane di Napoli* (nos. 92–95) ranges from light and open to dark and veiled. Macabre images of skulls, bodies, heads, and crosses tightly woven into a vague imaginary landscape cover the front page of the portfolio. Its figures are formed and surrounded by densely tangled but elegant black lines on a beige ground that fill the paper in a manner reminiscent of Jackson Pollock's allover drawings. Other prints in the suite elaborate on specific images depicted in the web of forms on the cover.

While similar in imagery to his prints, Paladino's paintings offer a less refined glimpse into the mystical world inhabited by his figures. *Le Tane di Napoli* (1983, no. 82), for instance, unlike the simple, linear quality of the etchings by that name, is heavily encrusted with roughly painted wooden crucifixes and other totemic wooden objects that extend the image beyond the canvas surface. It has an architectural framework. Large and heavy, it is barely contained by its massive frame. In contrast to his intimately scaled prints, this painting follows in the tradition of Italian church art, art meant for the public place. The ground of *Le Tane di Napoli* is formed by rich swirls of black, red and yellow offset by white. The effect is similar to that of Italian futurist paintings by Carlo Carrà or Luigi Russolo. Skulls and figures with the vacant expressionless stares and simplified bodies of Etruscan art peer out from the canvas, offsetting the painterly background. The elongation of the faces, frontality and mystical quality of forms reflect Paladino's knowledge of early Christian art. Besides evoking such early Italian precedents, *Le Tane di Napoli* is imbued with the myth and mystery associated with primitive art. Its solemn, masklike faces, strong raw colors, and wood reliefs recall the visages of Picasso's pre-cubist paintings and sculptures.

For Paladino, southern Italy, the area where he was born, continues to offer endless attraction. There, he says, "for centuries both the demonic and the religious have existed together without clear distinction." In light of this statement, perhaps the title *Le Tane di Napoli* refers to the many layers of civilization–the catacombs and Etruscan tombs–buried under present-day Naples. However, Paladino remarked in an interview with Danny Berger (*The Print Collector's Newsletter,* May–June 1983, p. 49) that in general, "the titles come to me much later. Sometimes years later. The titles really don't serve to identify the paintings or to help in the reading, but rather to create other poetic dimensions." His interest in Etruscan art appears to be a widespread and significant force in his work. In *Cometa delle Afriche* (1982, no. 81), for example, he lines the top and bottom edges with a frieze of bodies, skeletons, and indecipherable objects such as one might find in an Etruscan tomb. Similarly, the simply rendered stoic figure in the sculpture *Hortus Conclusus* (1982, no. 83) bears the aura of a mythical warrior, such as those depicted in Etruscan wall paintings or reliefs.

The manner in which Paladino makes use of his myriad sources reveals his versatility as a painter, sculptor and printmaker. His works are a brilliant synthesis of his observations of his own culture and its past, his knowledge and viewing of a tremendous variety of art forms, and the impressions he draws from his own imagination. Each one is an eclectic fusion of reality and dream, expressionism and anxious surrealism that ultimately veils each painting, print and sculpture in a mysterious haze.   FI

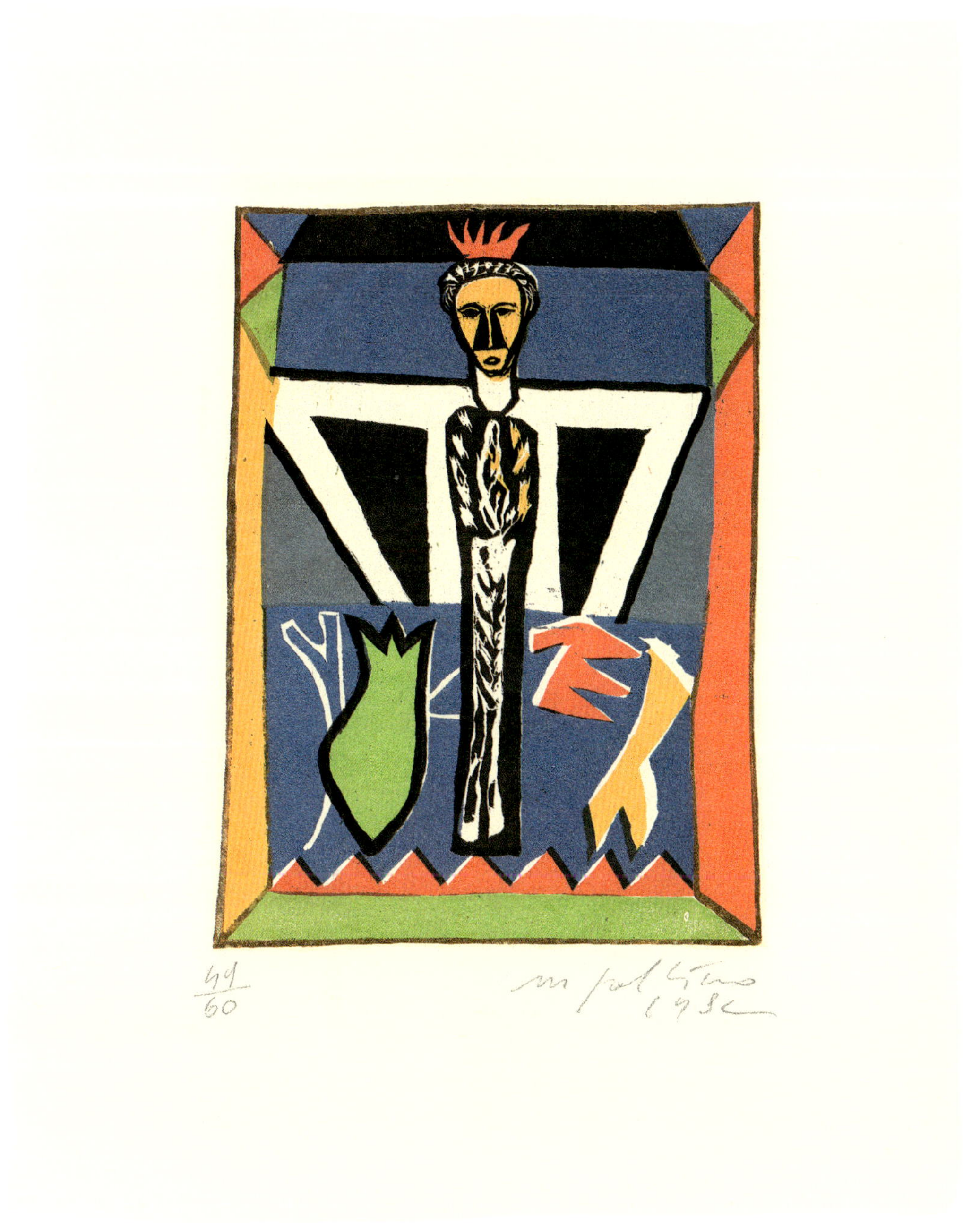

91. plate from *Bosforo* 1983

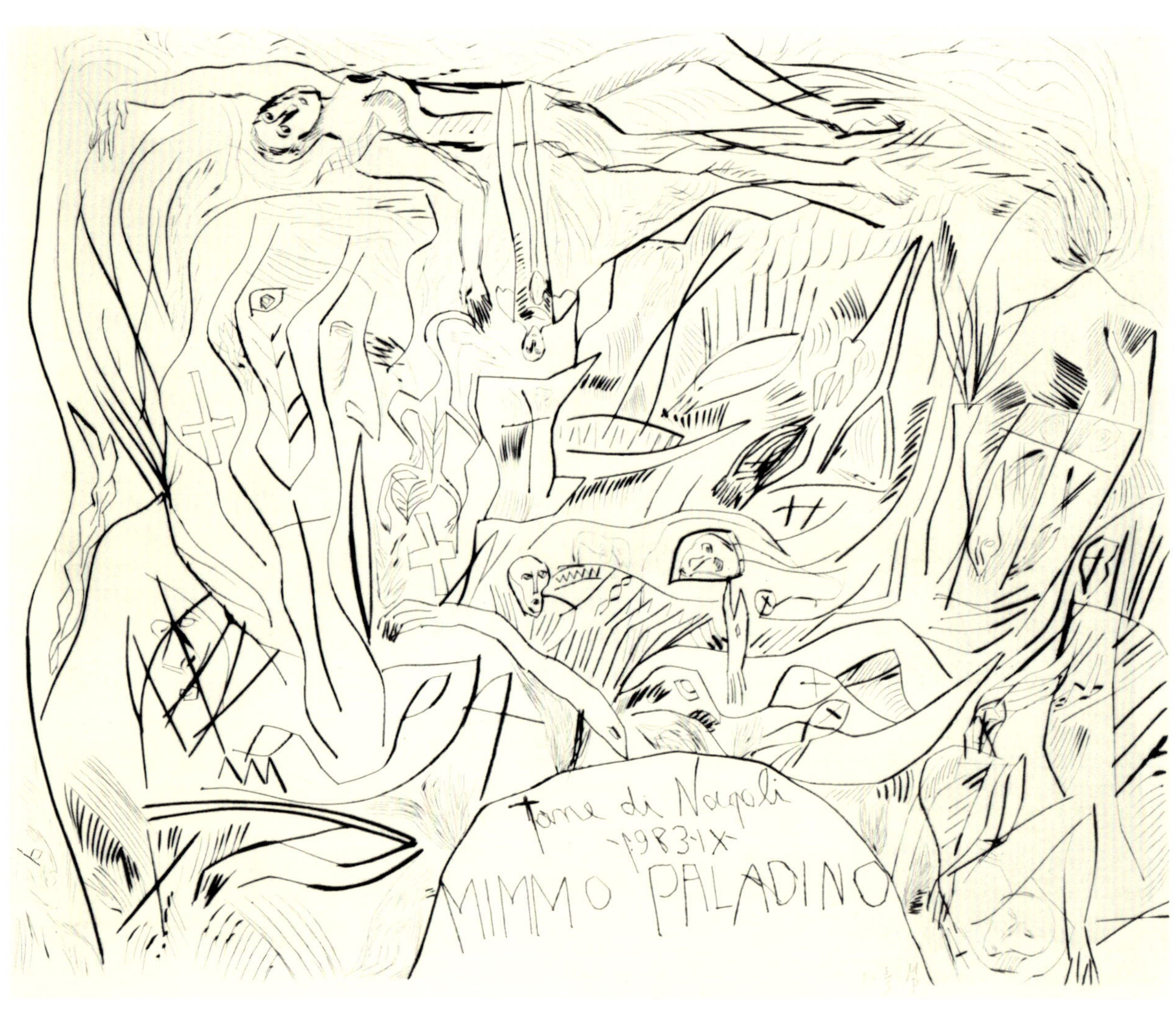

92. *Tane di Napoli* (cover) 1983

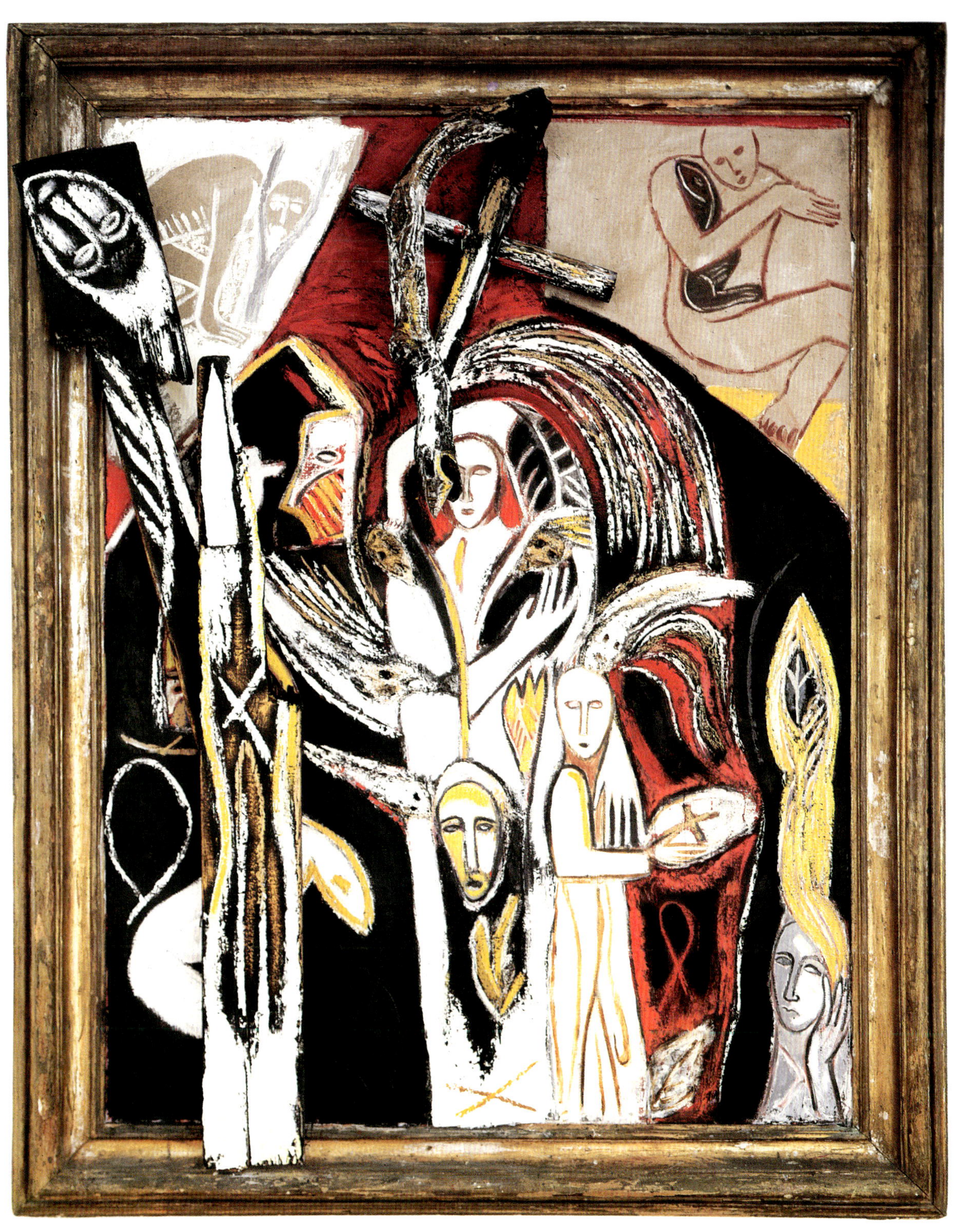

82. *Le Tane di Napoli* 1983

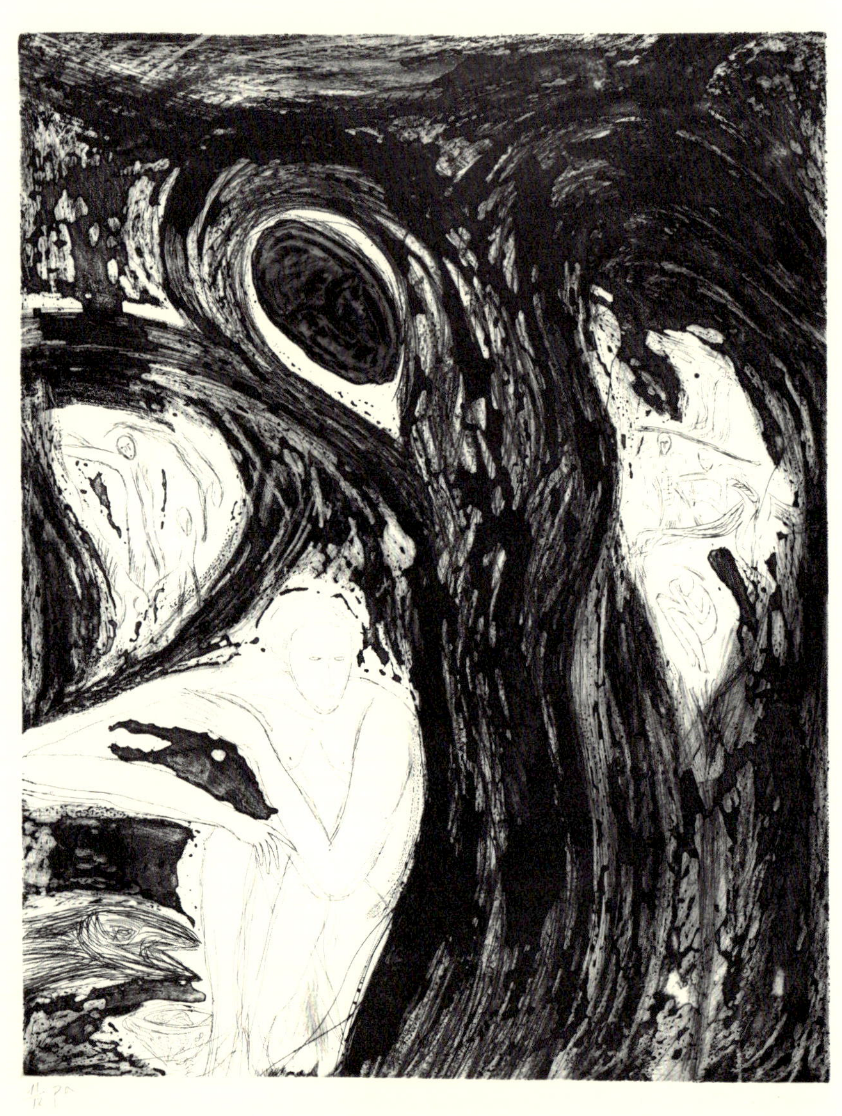

87. *Gocce nella Valle* 1982

MIMMO PALADINO

1948
Born in Paduli (Benevento), Italy
Lives in Milan and Benevento

Selected Solo Exhibitions
1977
Galleria dell'Ariete, Milan
Lucio Amelio, Naples
1978
Paul Maenz, Cologne, West Germany
Franco Toselli, Milan
1979
Lucio Amelio, Naples
Emilio Mazzoli, Modena, Italy
Art & Project, Amsterdam
1980
Paul Maenz, Cologne, West Germany
Annemarie Verna, Zürich, Switzerland
Badischer Kunstverein, Karlsruhe,
West Germany
Multiples/Marian Goodman, New York
Annina Nosei, New York
1981
Mario Diacono, Rome
Kunstmuseum Basel, Switzerland
Mannheimer Kunstverein, Mannheim,
West Germany
Groninger Museum, Groningen,
the Netherlands
Galleria d'Arte Moderna, Bologna, Italy
Franco Toselli, Milan
Bruno Bischofberger, Zürich, Switzerland
1982
Waddington Gallery, London
Louisiana Museum, Humlebaek, Denmark
Lucio Amelio, Naples
Multiples/Marian Goodman, New York
1983
Schellman & Kluser, Munich
Sperone Westwater, New York (catalogue)
Gian Enzo Sperone, Rome
1984
Galleria Toselli, Milan
Galerie Thomas, Munich

Selected Group Exhibitions
1979
Europa '79, Stuttgart, West Germany
Arte Cifra, Paul Maenz, Cologne,
West Germany
1980
Die Enthauptete Hand:
100 Zeichnungen aus Italien, Bonner
Kunstverein, Bonn, West Germany
Ego Navigatio, Mannheimer Kunstverein,
Mannheim, West Germany
Sieben junge Künstler aus Italien, Kunsthalle
Basel, Switzerland. Traveled to Museum
Folkwang, Essen, West Germany;
Stedelijk Museum, Amsterdam
Venice Biennale
1981
A New Spirit in Painting, Royal Academy
of Arts, London (catalogue)
Biennale de Paris

1982
4th Biennale of Sydney: Vision in Disbelief,
Sydney, Australia
Documenta 7, Kassel, West Germany
(catalogue)
Transavanguardia Internazionale, Galleria
Civica, Modena, Italy
Zeitgeist, Martin Gropius Bau, Berlin
(catalogue)
New Figuration from Europe, Milwaukee
Art Museum (catalogue)
1983
Italia: La Transavanguardia, Obra Culturel
de la Caja de Pensiones, Madrid
Tema Celeste, Museo Civico d'Arte
Contemporanea, Gibellina, Italy
*Concetto — Imago: Generationswechsel in
Italien*, Bonner Kunstverein, Bonn,
West Germany
Bilder der Angst und der Bedrohung,
Kunsthaus Zurich, Switzerland
Recent European Painting, The Solomon R.
Guggenheim Museum, New York
(catalogue)
New Art, The Tate Gallery, London
(catalogue)
1984
*Il Modo Italiano: Marisa Merz and Mimmo
Paladino*, Newport Harbor Art Museum,
Newport Beach, California (catalogue)
References, Palais des Beaux-Arts,
Charleroi, Belgium
*An International Survey of Recent Painting
and Sculpture*, The Museum of Modern Art,
New York (catalogue)

CHECKLIST

Paintings
81. *Cometa delle Afriche
(Comet of the Africas)* 1982
oil on canvas
108 x 108 (274.3 x 274.3)
Courtesy Sperone Westwater, New York
82. *Le Tane di Napoli
(The Hidden Places of Naples)* 1983
oil on canvas and wood collage
107¼ x 83¼ (272.4 x 211.5)
Collection Gerald S. Elliott, Chicago

Sculpture
83. *Hortus Conclusus
(Enclosed Garden)* 1982
bronze, patinas
80 x 60 x 56 (203.2 x 152.4 x 142.2)
Courtesy Sperone Westwater, New York

Prints
84. *Acqua di Stagno
(Water of the Pond)* 1980
etching, aquatint on paper; edition: 35
sheet and image: 22½ x 25 (57.2 x 63.5)
Courtesy Multiples, Inc., New York
85. *Con Musica
(With Music)* 1980
etching, aquatint, chine collé on paper;
edition: 35
sheet and image: 24¼ x 22 (61.6 x 55.9)
Courtesy Multiples, Inc., New York

86. *Figure Semplici
(Simple Figures)* 1982
drypoint, aquatint, modeling paste on
paper; edition: 60
image: 15¾ x 9½ (40 x 24)
sheet: 31 x 22½ (78.7 x 57.2)
Courtesy Sperone Westwater, New York
87. *Gocce nella Valle
(Drops in the Valley)* 1982
etching, aquatint, modeling paste on paper;
edition: 60
image: 25 x 19¼ (63.5 x 48.9)
sheet: 31 x 25½ (78.7 x 64.1)
Courtesy Sperone Westwater, New York
88. Untitled 1982
linocut, etching, aquatint on paper;
edition: 12
image: 23¼ x 19½ (59.1 x 49.5)
sheet: 31 x 22½ (78.7 x 57.2)
Courtesy Sperone Westwater, New York
89. Untitled 1982
etching, linocut on paper; edition: 12
image: 15⅞ x 10¾ (40.3 x 27.1)
sheet: 31 x 22½ (78.7 x 57.2)
Courtesy Sperone Westwater, New York
90. Untitled 1982
linocut, etching, aquatint on paper;
edition: 12
image: 15⅝ x 11¾ (39.7 x 29.9)
sheet: 31 x 22½ (78.7 x 57.2)
Courtesy Sperone Westwater, New York
91. *Bosforo (Bosforus)* 1983
six wood engravings in book form;
edition: 60
one image: 8⅛ x 6 (20.7 x 15.3)
one image: 5⅜ x 2⅝ (13.5 x 6.5)
four images: 5½ x 7 (14 x 17.8)
sheet: 13 x 10¼ each (33 x 26)
Courtesy Sperone Westwater, New York
92–95. *Tane di Napoli
(Hidden Places of Naples)* 1983
portfolio of three drypoints on
paper with cover; edition: 33
cover: 19¼ x 23¼ (49.8 x 59.1)
image: 9⅝ x 12⅝ each (24.3 x 32)
sheet: 19¼ x 23¼ (49.8 x 59.1)
Courtesy Sperone Westwater, New York
96–99. Untitled 1983
four line etchings with aquatint, and two
with drypoint on paper;
edition: to be determined
image: 6⅝ x 7¾ (16.8 x 19.7)
sheet: 14½ x 15¾ (36.8 x 40)
Courtesy Sperone Westwater, New York
100–103. Untitled 1984
portfolio of four linocuts drawn from
James Joyce's *Ulysses*; edition: 65
image: 31⅞ x 47⅝ each (81 x 121)
sheet: 38⅛ x 53⅛ each (97 x 135)
Courtesy Dolan/Maxwell, Philadelphia
Dedalus
Ellpodbomool
Introibo ad Altare Dei
Sogno Umido

SUSAN ROTHENBERG

Susan Rothenberg has said that the primary motivation for her printmaking is the opportunity it affords to break the isolation of the painting studio, an increasingly private sanctuary for the artist. This modest comment belies her impressive achievements in printmaking; she has already explored various techniques, among them lithography, aquatint, woodcut and drypoint. Moreover, the sense of extreme isolation that characterizes Rothenberg's painting imagery is also evident in her prints, despite the presence of other people during the process of their creation.

Rothenberg has made nearly twenty prints since 1977, and the subject matter in all of them bears an intimate relationship to the themes of her paintings. The image of the horse, which has appeared in her work since 1974, similarly appears in her prints. *Tattoo* (1979, no. 104), one of Rothenberg's late horse paintings, characteristically portrays the animal and its various components in a highly ambiguous manner. The blue horse with its vague boundaries contrasts with two legs on either side, resolutely defined by thick black lines, though curiously upside down. The title, *Tattoo*, refers to the horse's head drawn into the leg, "a tattoo or memory image," as the artist describes it, whose illogical presence further violates our sense of order. It is not readily apparent which direction the horse is facing. It stands on the milky field like a creature lost in a blinding snowstorm, the pathways on either side, other facets of itself, its only bearings. Rothenberg has said of *Tattoo*, "It has elements that I think will be in my work all my life: hollows and solids, shallow space, mystery, the disembodied quality. I can't tell you why but the painting sits right with me. On the surface, I can say that it's well-built; it has the right color in the right place on the right form in the right combination of black and white."

In a number of her prints based on the horse image, there is a dramatic shift in the way Rothenberg combines black and white. Untitled *(May #4)* (1979, no. 110) and *Four Rays* (1980–83, no. 117) both have a solid black ground not found in her paintings where, in the artist's words, "there is no square foot of black that isn't beaten up with gray and white to activate the ground." The plight of the horse struggling to emerge from the dark, dense field parallels our own struggle to discern its image or meaning. Untitled *(May #1)* (1979, no. 107), another horse image, shares with *Tattoo* the opposition of solid and hollow, the hollow legs embracing the shadowy horse and providing the same dizzying perspective implied by their upside-down configuration.

In the series of "head and hand" paintings that followed the horses, Rothenberg again sketched a broad outline, leaving the viewer to fill in many of the details. Her juxtaposed image of head and hand made its first appearance in a 1980 series of unique woodcuts titled *Pinks* (nos. 113–115). The more intimate scale of printmaking provided the artist with the freedom to experiment, and the series proved to be a breakthrough. As she noted: "I was thinking that all I have is a head and a hand to paint with, and eyes in my head." Her use of pink and black enhances the devilish quality of *Pinks*, as do the fingers pointing upward, resembling devil's horns. In the series of five paintings that followed, the mouth vanished and the eyes were filled in. The image became schematic, primitive, and the reference to the universal childhood activity of tracing one's hand, an early venture in self-discovery, grew stronger. The untitled head and hand painting of 1980–81 (no. 105) has a dark field, unlike the other paintings in this group. Rothenberg refers to it as her "night painting." Its orbital orange and green rings, forming a holding device, locate the image in outer space, and the Halloween palette gives the painting an eerie cast.

The imagery in Rothenberg's recent work is increasingly diverse. Figures engaged in a variety of activities from boating to making love are portrayed in a thicket of brushstrokes that Rothenberg marvelously terms "the weather." Light and movement have become paramount concerns, and sound, implied in earlier works (the horse pacing, the series of heads emitting "talk"), is evoked in the newer work as well. The whoosh of sailboats and swans gliding across water, and water cascading from a bucket, all recent subjects, provide a subliminally soothing note, in contrast to the screams of Edvard Munch, an artist with whom Rothenberg is frequently compared.

Rothenberg's recent engagement with the larger world comes as a relief. Moving from symbol to reality, she has begun to investigate a wider sphere of human activity, bringing to that challenge the analytic intensity that has always characterized her work. The same restraint in conveying information about what is going on prevails, as in recent paintings such as *Mist from the Chest* (1983, no. 106) and in prints such as *Puppet* (1983, no. 119). In the painting an odd figure reappears, its detached, pluglike head a familiar form. It is difficult to discern what is happening to the figure, which is awkwardly poised at a 45-degree angle to the ground. Her woodblock *Puppet* features a figure with the same detached, pluglike head; rather than being grounded, however awkwardly, this body is suspended in darkness by two lines, suggesting a puppet, as the title implies, or the victim of a hanging. One can never be certain with Rothenberg, especially in her prints, where her reticence reaches its extreme. One's own effort to identify the attenuated image in *Puppet* parallels the struggles in which Rothenberg's figures are engaged.   MG

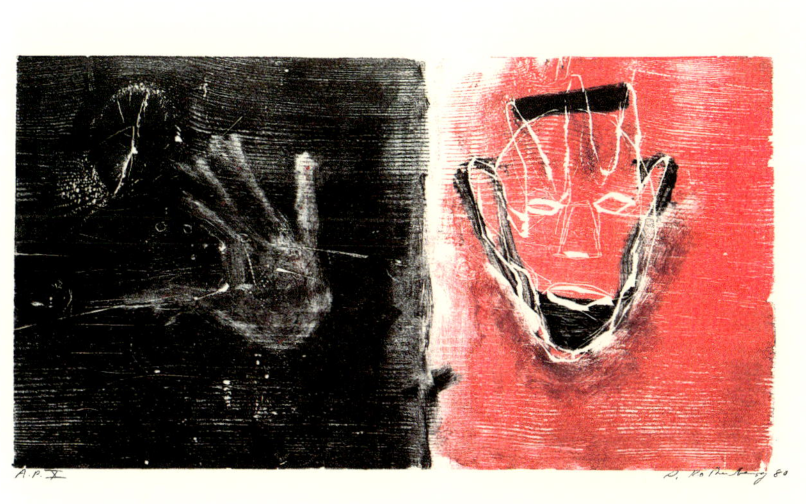

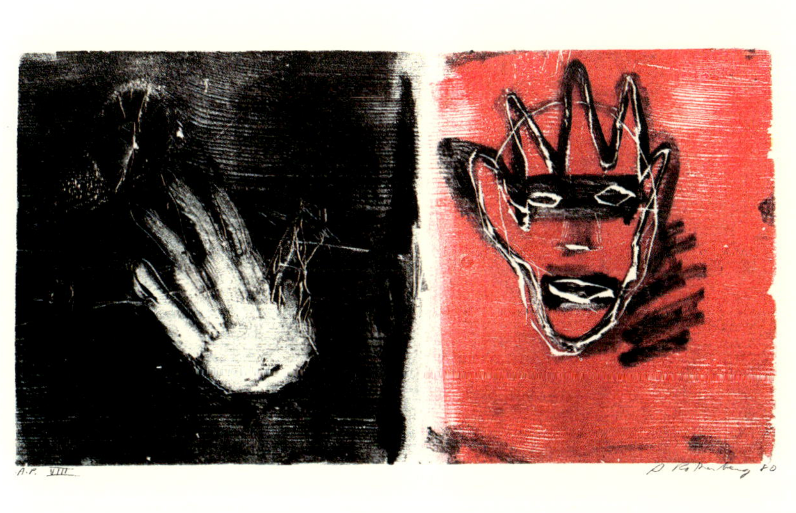

114–115. *Pinks* 1980

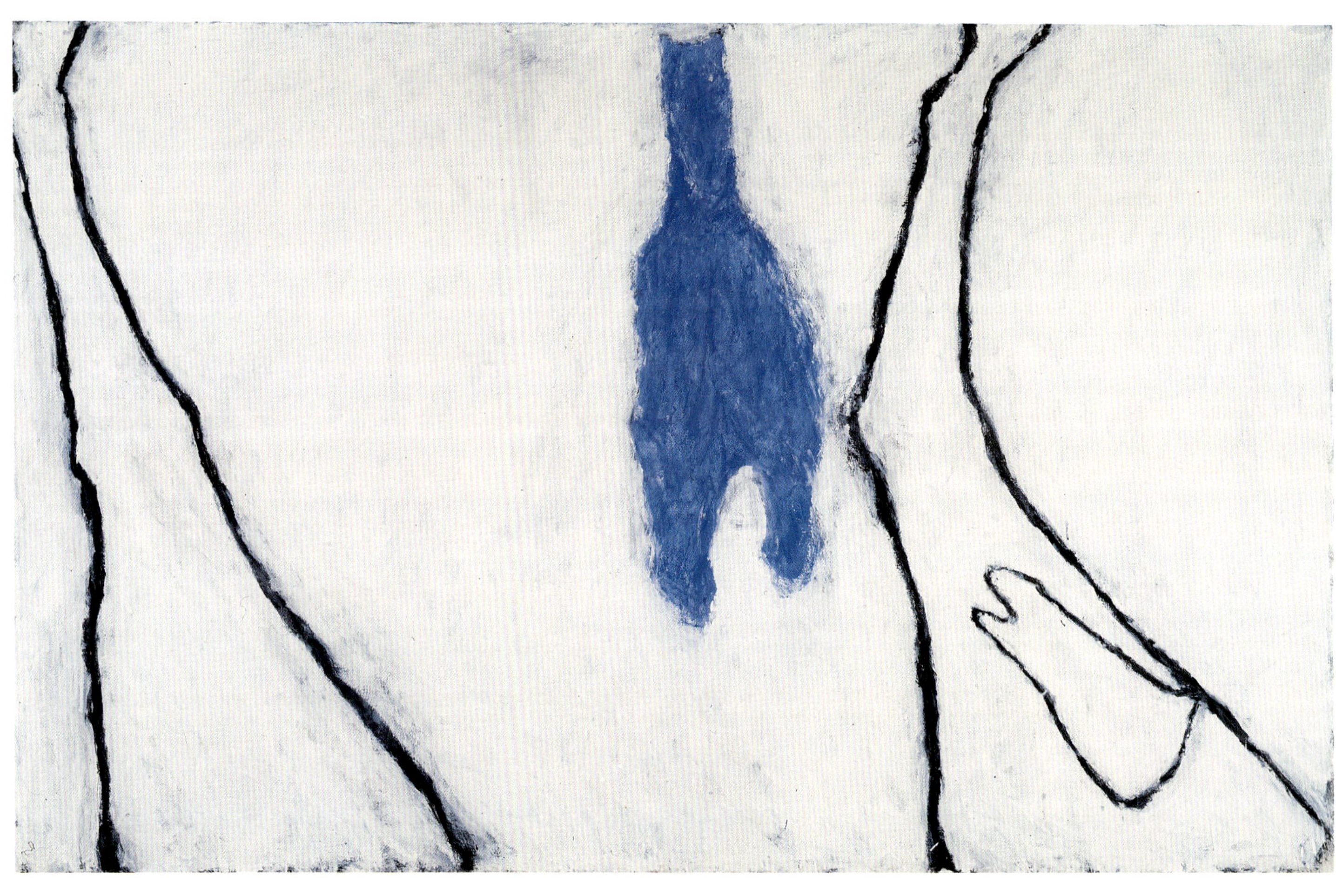

104. *Tattoo* 1979

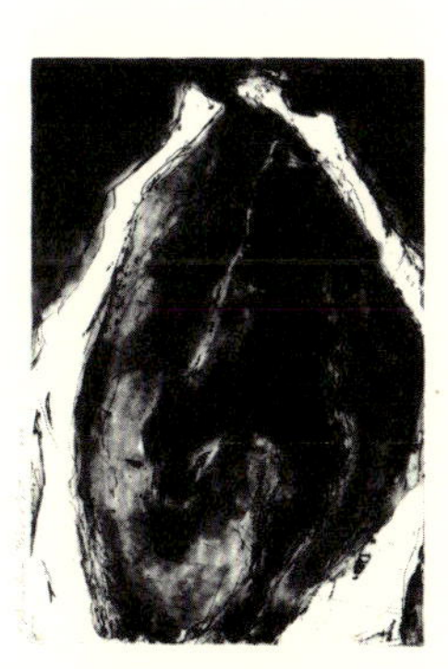

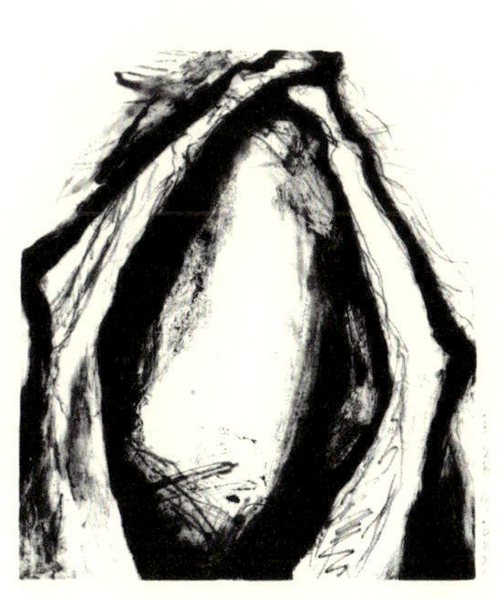

107. Untitled *(May #1)* 1979 (top)
108. Untitled *(May #2)* 1979

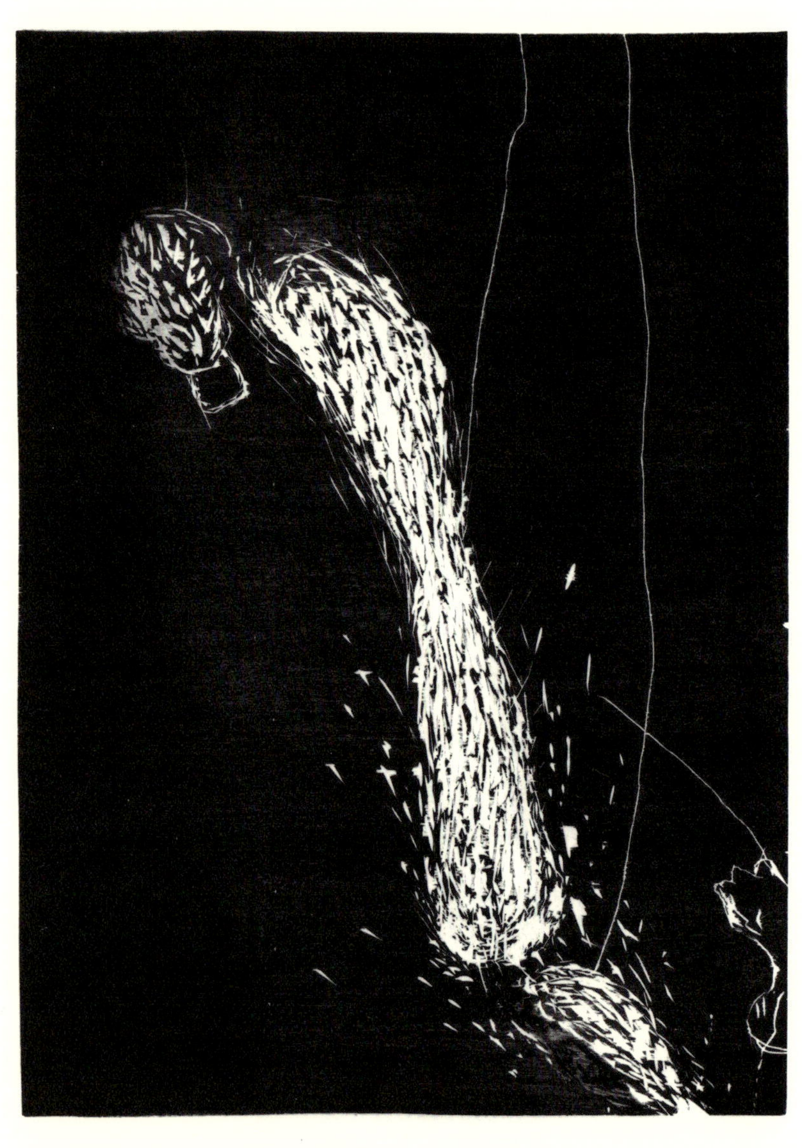

119. *Puppet* 1983

SUSAN ROTHENBERG

1945
Born in Buffalo, New York
1967
B.F.A. Cornell University, Ithaca,
New York
Lives in New York

Solo Exhibitions
1975
Three Large Paintings, 112 Greene Street
Gallery, New York
1976
Willard Gallery, New York
1977
Willard Gallery, New York
1978
Viewpoints, Walker Art Center,
Minneapolis
Matrix, University Art Museum,
University of California, Berkeley
Greenberg Gallery, St. Louis
1979
Willard Gallery, New York
1980
Mayor Gallery, London
Galerie Rudolph Zwirner, Cologne,
West Germany
1981
Five Heads, Willard Gallery, New York
Akron Art Museum, Ohio
1982
Stedelijk Museum, Amsterdam (catalogue)
1983
Willard Gallery, New York
Gallery 6: Susan Rothenberg, Los Angeles
County Museum of Art. Traveled to
San Francisco Museum of Modern Art;
Museum of Art, Carnegie Institute,
Pittsburgh; Institute of Contemporary Art,
Boston (brochure)
1984
Susan Rothenberg Prints 1977 – 1984,
Barbara Krakow Gallery, Boston
(catalogue)

Selected Group Exhibitions
1976
New Work/New York, Fine Arts Gallery,
California State University, Los Angeles
1979
Visionary Images, Renaissance Society at
the University of Chicago (catalogue)
1979 Biennial Exhibition, Whitney
Museum of American Art, New York
(catalogue)
American Painting: The Eighties, Grey Art
Gallery, New York University, New York
1980
Painting and Sculpture Today 1980,
Indianapolis Museum of Art (catalogue)
Venice Biennale, International and United
States Pavilions (catalogue)
1981
*Robert Moskowitz, Susan Rothenberg,
Julian Schnabel,* Kunsthalle Basel,
Switzerland. Traveled to Frankfurter
Kunstverein, Frankfurt, West Germany;
Louisiana Museum, Humlebaek, Denmark
(catalogue)

1982
Zeitgeist, Martin Gropius Bau, Berlin
(catalogue)
74th American Exhibition, The Art Institute
of Chicago (catalogue)
New Figuration in America, Milwaukee Art
Museum (catalogue)
Focus on the Figure: Twenty Years, Whitney
Museum of American Art, New York
(catalogue)
Block Prints, Whitney Museum of American
Art, New York (brochure)
1983
Tendencias en Nueva York,
Palacio de Cristal, Madrid (catalogue)
Prints from Blocks: Gauguin to Now,
The Museum of Modern Art, New York
(catalogue)
1983 Biennial Exhibition, Whitney
Museum of American Art, New York
(catalogue)
*Drawing Conclusions: A Survey of
American Drawing, 1958 – 1983,* Daniel
Weinberg Gallery, Los Angeles
Back to the U.S.A., Kunstmuseum Luzern,
Lucerne, Switzerland (catalogue)
American Accents Américains, Gallery
Stratford, Ontario (catalogue)
1984
*An International Survey of Recent Painting
and Sculpture,* The Museum of Modern Art,
New York (catalogue)

CHECKLIST

Paintings
104. *Tattoo* 1979
acrylic, flasche on canvas
67 x 103 (170.2 x 261.6)
Collection Walker Art Center, Minneapolis
Purchased with the aid of funds from
Mr. and Mrs. Edmond R. Ruben, Mr. and
Mrs. Julius E. Davis, Art Center Acquisition
Fund and the National Endowment for the
Arts
105. Untitled 1980 – 81
acrylic, flasche on canvas
104 x 114 (264.2 x 289.6)
Collection Munson-Williams-Proctor
Institute, Utica, New York
106. *Mist from the Chest* 1983
oil on canvas
78 x 89 (198.1 x 226.1)
Collection Milwaukee Art Museum,
Gift of Friends of Art

Prints
107. Untitled *(May #1)* 1979
etching on paper; edition: 45
image: 11¾ x 8 (29.8 x 20.3)
sheet: 29½ x 22 (74.9 x 55.9)
Courtesy Willard Gallery, New York
108. Untitled *(May #2)* 1979
etching on paper; edition: 45
image: 13¾ x 11¾ (34.9 x 29.8)
sheet: 29½ x 22 (74.9 x 55.9)
Courtesy Willard Gallery, New York

109. Untitled *(May #3)* 1979
etching on paper; edition: 45
image: 23¾ x 17½ (60.3 x 44.5)
sheet: 29⅝ x 22 (75.2 x 55.9)
Courtesy Willard Gallery, New York
110. Untitled *(May #4)* 1979
etching on paper; edition: 45
image: 23¾ x 17½ (60.3 x 44.5)
sheet: 29⅝ x 22 (75.2 x 55.9)
Courtesy Willard Gallery, New York
111. *Head and Bones* 1980
woodcut on paper; edition: 20
image: 13 x 11¼ (33 x 28.6)
sheet: 25½ x 18¼ (64.8 x 46.4)
Collection The Minneapolis
Institute of Arts
The Ethel Morrison Van Derlip Fund
112. *Head and Hand* 1980
woodcut on paper; edition: 15
image: 13 x 11¼ (33 x 28.6)
sheet: 25½ x 18¼ (65.4 x 46.4)
Courtesy Multiples, Inc., New York
113. *Pinks* 1980
hand-painted woodcut on paper;
edition: 20
image: 11⅛ x 20 (28.3 x 50.8)
sheet: 19 x 27 (48.3 x 58)
Courtesy Multiples, Inc., New York
114. *Pinks* 1980
hand-painted woodcut on paper;
edition: 20
image: 11⅛ x 20 (28.3 x 50.8)
sheet: 19 x 27 (48.3 x 58)
Courtesy Multiples, Inc., New York
115. *Pinks* 1980
hand-painted woodcut on paper;
edition: 20
image: 11⅛ x 20 (28.3 x 50.8)
sheet: 19 x 27 (48.3 x 58)
Courtesy Multiples, Inc., New York
116. *Five-Color Wishbone* 1980 – 81
lithograph on paper; edition: 26
sheet and image: 25 x 25½ (63.5 x 64.8)
Courtesy Willard Gallery, New York
117. *Four Rays* 1980 – 83
lithograph, acidtint on paper; edition: 34
image: 10 x 14 (25.4 x 35.6)
sheet: 21 x 24 (53.3 x 61)
Courtesy Willard Gallery, New York
118. *Plug* 1983
lithograph on paper; edition: 29
sheet and image: 30 x 22 (76.2 x 55.9)
Courtesy John C. Stoller & Co.,
Minneapolis
119. *Puppet* 1983
woodcut on paper; edition: 25
image: two blocks, 48 x 33¾ each
(121.9 x 85.7)
sheet: 70 x 37 (177.8 x 94)
Collection First Bank Minneapolis
120. *Between the Eyes* 1984
hand-painted lithograph, woodcut,
collage on paper; edition: 36
sheet and image: 57½ x 34 (146.1 x 86.4)
Collection Romuald Tecco, Minneapolis
121. *Four Green Lines* 1984
lithograph on paper; edition: 30
image: 22 x 30 (55.9 x 76.2)
sheet: 30½ x 35 (77.5 x 88.9)
Courtesy Willard Gallery, New York

T. L. SOLIEN

T. L. Solien is a storyteller who readily acknowledges the autobiographical content of his work. His harsh, barren landscape is not unlike the flat Midwestern countryside of Minnesota, where he was raised and prefers to live. In the format of his drawings and paintings of the late 1970s, consisting of pictographic symbols against solid fields of color, he attempted to synthesize aspects of Abstract Expressionism and Minimalism. Uncomfortable with the abbreviated, shorthand nature of the results, he began fleshing out his spare pictographs, describing the images in an identifiable fashion, giving the figures color, dimension and specific attributes, and generally imparting a narrative flavor to the work. Since 1980, Solien has developed a confident and consistent style in which a recurring cast of characters, among them the tin man, the jester and the Mouseketeer, inhabit an eerie landscape, its ominous skies filled with tears and curious floating orbs representing an emotional counterpoint to the thoughts and dreams of the earthbound figures below.

The Straw Ox (1984, no. 124) is based on the children's story about an impoverished farmer and his wife who construct a straw ox to capture for sustenance animals who roam the forest. Drawn to the decoy, the unfortunate beasts stick to its tar-covered surface. According to the tale, in exchange for their freedom, the captive animals promise to supply the couple with domestic animals–ducks, chickens, goats and the like– for their food. In Solien's painting the ox shares the stage with a sad-faced tin man, a frequent protagonist in the artist's work recalling the *Wizard of Oz* character. The enigmatic scene suggests a Samuel Beckett vignette–two woebegone characters, one precariously held together with baling wire, the other with nails. Though the tin man looks vaguely human, he of course has no heart and lacks the capacity to feel. He looks to the ox for the means of survival, just as the couple in the story did. One can speculate that the tin man represents the artist, who seeks salvation in painting, for which the straw ox serves as a metaphor. The orange sphere suspended above the ox contains what may be a dove with an olive branch. Although the bird's form resembles a teardrop and the branch is bare and spindly, surely this subplot stands as a symbol for hope.

Self-revelation and struggle as well as storytelling are characteristic of Solien's painting; they are also evident in his printmaking. Portraits of the artist and his family appear in his two edition prints *The*

Nightwatchman (1982, no. 133) and *The Three Sailors* (1982, no. 134) and his suite of drypoint etchings *Fragments of Hope* (1982, nos. 127–132). Beguiled by the primitive rendering of images in the etchings, which range from a man in a Mickey Mouse hat to a snowman, on close inspection one feels the poignancy of the event that prompted the series, the loss of an infant child, represented by the cone-shaped figure in swaddling clothes. Life's burdens (symbolized in these prints by the rock piles), the precarious balances in family relationships and the fragility of life itself are Solien's concerns. To portray them, he has drawn from a reservoir of personal symbols, among them the tooth, the diamond and the candle. The candle, traditionally a sign of knowledge, has a specific association for Solien: it reminds him of a song he sang as a child in Bible class, which likened faith to a candle one should fearlessly allow to shine. Whatever the original source of his image and however private its meaning for him, he harnesses it in the service of telling a story that touches us all.

Solien's most gruesome images appear in his monotypes: skulls, a fish head on a spit, a toothless ox head, sheared-off limbs. The struggles that preoccupy the artist in all his work are immediately apparent in these prints, such as *Victim of Doubt* (1983, no. 137), which are stripped of the mitigating charm of fairytale images. Solien may spend from a week to a month on a painting, whereas a monotype may require only a half-hour to complete. The immediacy of the process enables him to work in an uninhibited fashion–before self-editing begins–allowing him to vent his fiercest and most primitive feelings fully. He is especially attracted to the transparency inherent in the monotype process, a result of the paper's inability to draw all the ink off the plate, and has sought to endow his subsequent canvases with similar light.

Although Solien has drawn on surrealist painting conventions, borrowing notably from Miró, his compositions are more deliberate, less marked by the spontaneity of Surrealism. The grotesque and exaggerated aspects of Solien's imagery, particularly the cartoonlike character of his works on paper, may be compared to the late paintings of Philip Guston. Ultimately, Solien speaks in his own voice; resonating with religious overtones, his work speaks of the struggle to maintain one's faith and the search for meaning in life.   MG

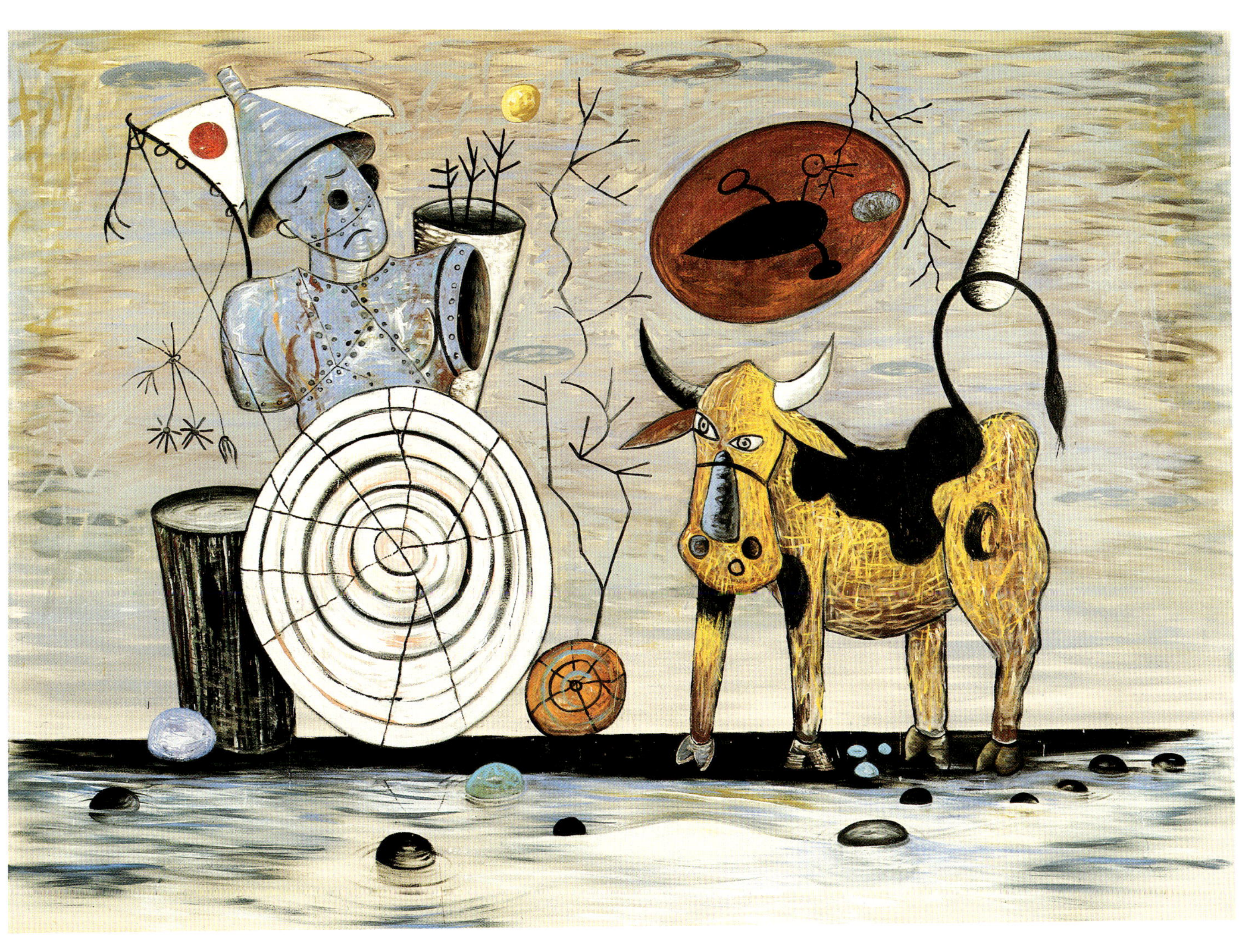

124. *The Straw Ox* 1984

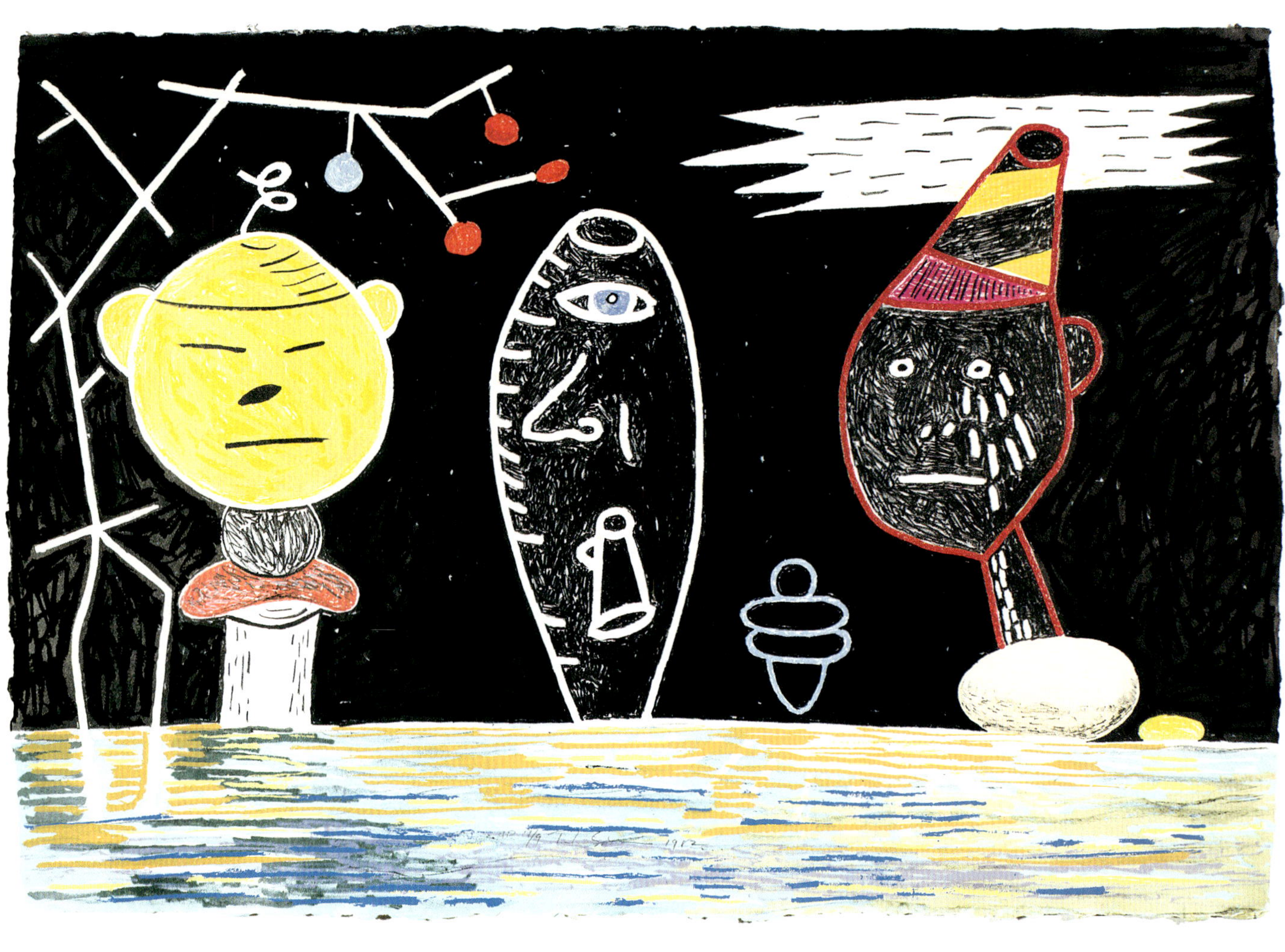

134. *The Three Sailors* 1982

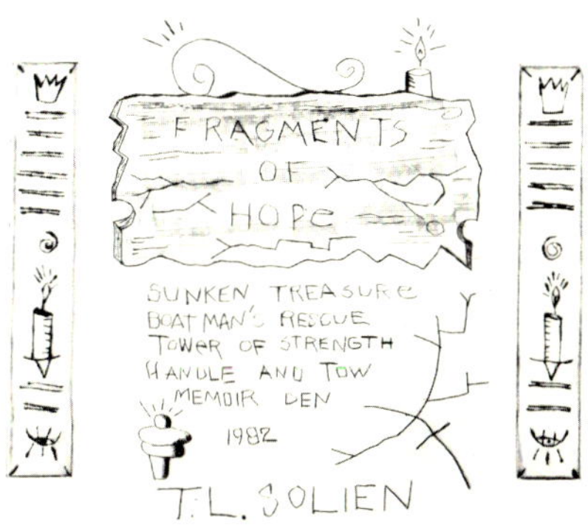

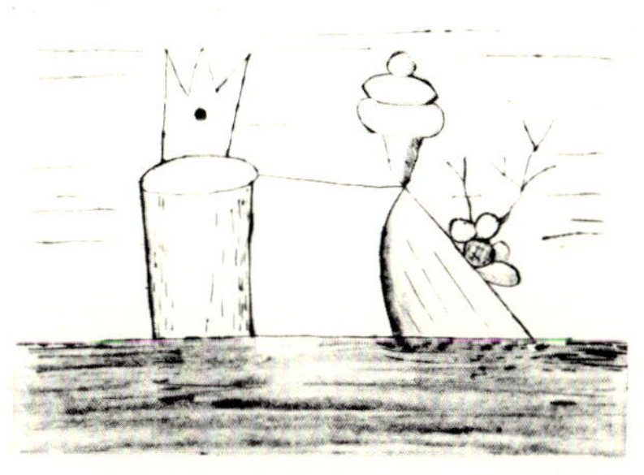
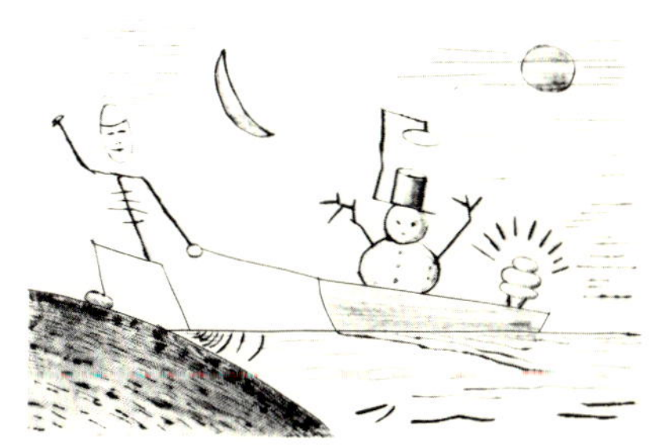
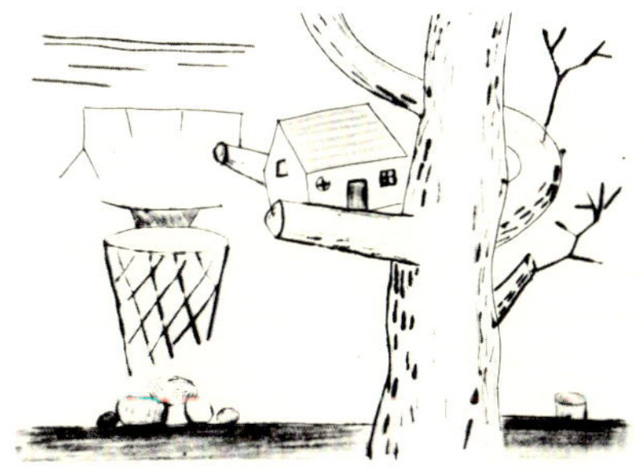
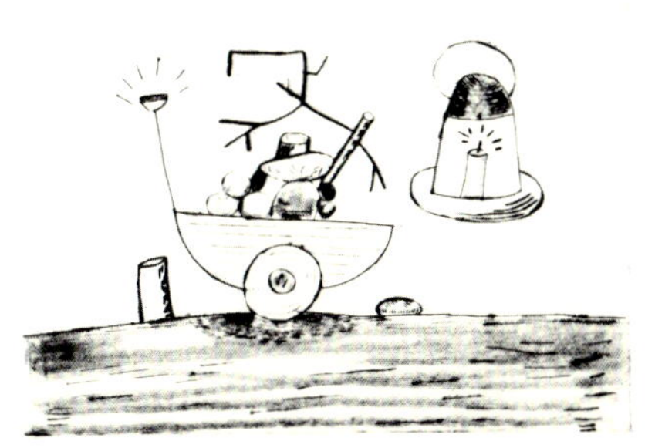
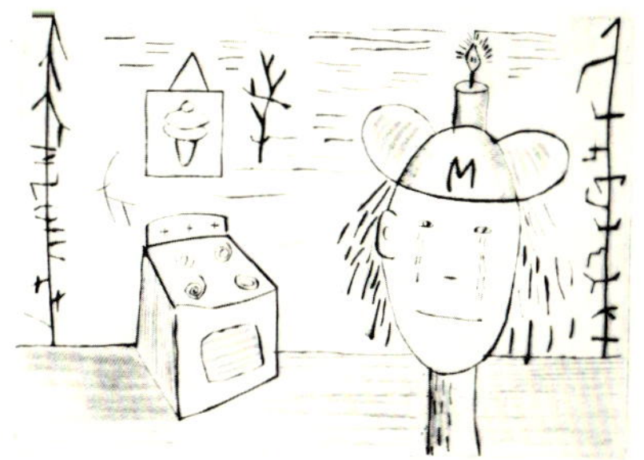

127–132.   *Fragments of Hope*   1982

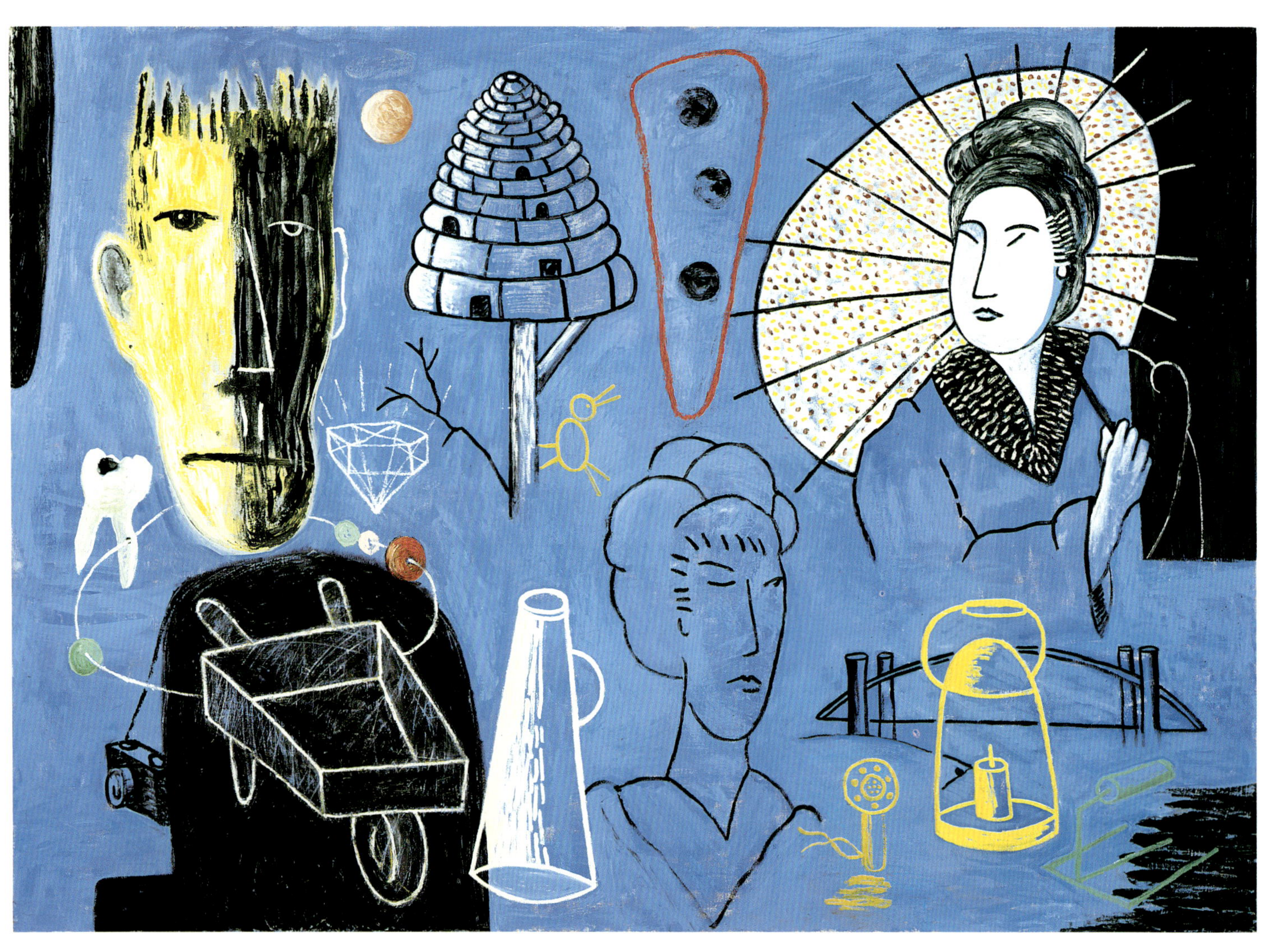

123. *Bricklayer's Tender* 1983

1949
Born in Fargo, North Dakota
1973
B.F.A., Moorhead State University,
Moorhead, Minnesota
1977
M.F.A., University of Nebraska, Lincoln
Lives in Pelican Rapids, Minnesota

Solo Exhibitions
1979
Glen Hanson Gallery, Minneapolis
*Blue Day on Earth: Tell a Lie to Tell the
Truth*, Minneapolis College of Art and
Design (catalogue)
1980
Glen Hanson Gallery, Minneapolis
The Prodigal Son, The Fort Worth
Art Museum (brochure)
1983
Les Pierres du Minnesota, American Center,
Paris
Getler/Pall Gallery, New York
van Straaten Gallery, Chicago
1984
Cantor/Lemberg Gallery, Birmingham,
Michigan
Getler/Pall/Saper, New York

Selected Group Exhibitions
1977
Nebraska Drawings, Syracuse University,
Syracuse, New York
1980
Prints and Multiples, Glen Hanson Gallery,
Minneapolis
*Ten Minnesota Artists Represented by the
Glen Hanson Gallery*, Schaeffer Art Gallery,
Gustavus Adolphus College, St. Peter,
Minnesota
1981
Drawing Invitational, Glen Hanson Gallery,
Minneapolis
Minneapolis II, Dayton's Gallery 12,
Minneapolis
General Mills Art Collection, Loch Haven
Center, Orlando, Florida
1982
The Bewildered Image, The Minneapolis
Institute of Arts
1983
1983 Biennial Exhibition, Whitney
Museum of American Art, New York
(catalogue)
*The American Artist as Printmaker:
Twenty-third National Print Exhibition*,
The Brooklyn Museum, New York
(catalogue)
1984
Painting Invitational, Rutgers University,
Campus at Newark, New Jersey
Rooted in North Dakota, North Dakota
Museum of Art, Grand Forks

CHECKLIST

Paintings
122.   *Jewels of the Knitting Man*   1982
oil on canvas
66 x 54 (167.6 x 137.2)
Private Collection
123.   *Bricklayer's Tender*   1983
oil on canvas
66 x 90 (167.6 x 228.6)
Collection Walker Art Center, Minneapolis
Jerome Foundation Purchase Fund for
Emerging Artists
124.   *The Straw Ox*   1984
oil, enamel, alkyd on canvas
84 x 114 (213.2 x 296)
Collection the artist

Drawings
125.   *All That Glitters Is Not Gold*
1982
flasche on paper
23 x 30 (54.8 x 76.2)
Collection First Bank Minneapolis
126.   *The Fool Escapes Death by
Pretending*   1982 – 83
flasche on paper
22 x 30 (55.9 x 76.2)
Courtesy Getler/Pall/Saper Gallery,
New York

Prints
127 – 132.   *Fragments of Hope*   1982
portfolio of six drypoints on paper;
edition: 21
sheet: 13¼ x 17¼ each (33.7 x 43.8)
Courtesy Vermillion Editions Ltd.,
Minneapolis
Title Page
image: 10¾ x 10¾ (27.4 x 27.4)
I Sunken Treasure
image: 7¾ x 10¾ (19.8 x 27.4)
II Boatman's Rescue
image: 7¾ x 11 (19.8 x 27.9)
III Tower of Strength
image: 7¾ x 10¾ (19.8 x 27.4)
IV Handle and Tow
image: 7¾ x 11 (19.8 x 27.9)
V Memoir Den
image: 8 x 10¾ (20.4 x 27.4)
133.   *The Nightwatchman*   1982
lithograph, intaglio, screen print on paper;
edition: 18
sheet and image: diptych, 20 x 22½ each
(50.8 x 57.2)
Courtesy Vermillion Editions Ltd.,
Minneapolis
134.   *The Three Sailors*   1982
lithograph, screen print on paper;
edition: 43
sheet and image: 32½ x 46½ (82.6 x 118.1)
Courtesy Vermillion Editions Ltd.,
Minneapolis

135.   *At the Foot of the Cross*   1983
monotype on paper
sheet and image: 30½ x 41 (77.5 x 104.1)
Courtesy Vermillion Editions Ltd.,
Minneapolis
136.   *History of Broken Arrows*   1983
monotype on paper
sheet and image: 30 x 40 (76.2 x 101.6)
Collection Dr. and Mrs. Mitchell Sheinkop,
Chicago
137.   *Victim of Doubt*   1983
monotype on paper
sheet and image: 30½ x 41 (77.5 x 104.1)
BankAmerica Corporation Art Collection,
San Francisco
138.   *The Tin Man*   1984
monotype on paper
sheet and image: 41 x 31 (104.1 x 78.7)
Courtesy Vermillion Editions Ltd.,
Minneapolis

DONALD SULTAN

In his art, Donald Sultan has surveyed the American industrial landscape since the mid-1970s. His images range from factories to streetlamps, from telephone poles to oil pumps; they all point toward the artist's abiding concern with how things get made and his fascination with the very underpinnings of the industrial age. While his paintings reflect the general shift from abstraction to representational imagery pursued by many of his generation, Sultan's work is focussed on external emblems of today's culture rather than on probings of an internal or personal nature.

His paintings of factories, dating from 1976, are typical of the way in which the artist approaches his subject matter and have spawned many of his subsequent series. Constructed from linoleum floor tile, they make witty reference to the history of modern painting with their declaredly flat surface as they feature the world beyond his studio, a cityscape cluttered with smokestacks, the modern urban equivalent to the forest. Yet these paintings also refer to his own immediate environment, a studio in which the main element is the table: flipped upside down, the factory's smokestacks read as table legs. The artist suggests the creative possibilities inherent in the industrial and vice versa. This strategy of exploring contradictions in forms while searching for their common ground is a central characteristic of Sultan's work.

Over the years the smokestack image has evolved into a flower shape in works such as *Yellow Iris/ Smokestack, May–June 1981* (no. 139), and into a cigarette (the smokestack tipped 90 degrees) in a series of paintings. The smoking cigarette, a human-scale version of a smokestack, first emerged in a portfolio of eight aquatints titled *Water Under the Bridge*, printed in 1979. This extraordinary metamorphosis of imagery was followed most recently by the transformation of the smokestack/flower/cigarette image into the fire-breathing guns of a battleship, another one of the symbols of power which the artist frequently depicts. Sultan hangs on to images the way other people hold on to the everyday items of their past. Instead of harboring useless items in the attic, however, Sultan recycles them, and each time an image reappears, it is all the richer for its associations with earlier incarnations.

Sultan makes art with linoleum tile, plaster and tar, all "nonart" materials. Traditionally used in industrial processes, these media are particularly well-suited to his observations on the urban condition. He affixes the linoleum tile to Masonite, supporting it from behind with stretcher bars. He draws on the tile, and with a blowtorch softens certain areas, scraping away the surface and filling it with either tar or plaster, which is then painted over. The larger works are composed of two or four panels, joined together in a manner that clearly manifests their multipartite construction. The medium and the method are a significant part of the message in these works: he puns on the ingredients of cigarettes by using tar in the cigarette series, and the flames in the forest fire paintings are a reference to the method of their creation, which involves the use of a torch.

Sultan has pursued the tulip image, another successor to the slender smokestack, for several years. In 1983 he completed a suite of aquatints entitled *Black Tulips* (nos. 152–155), and his series of large and imposing charcoal drawings of tulips (nos. 141–143) is ongoing. In form and chronology the tulip paintings parallel his paintings of old-fashioned gooseneck streetlamps. Moving back and forth among the various media, he emphasizes the special qualities of each; all the while the work is informed by his fascination with the numerous ways an image can be read and the paradoxes that lie therein.

The tulip paintings are a bridge between natural and industrial forms and between figuration and abstraction. The yellow bulb of the tulip paintings is also the flame emerging from the smokestack, just as the angular petal is also the factory rooftop. The title *Yellow Iris/ Smokestack, May–June 1981* makes explicit the image's borderline position. In contrast to the rigid and erect aspect of the paintings, the charcoal drawings tend toward graceful curves and erotic forms. They have a distinguished formal heritage in the draftsmanship of Henri Matisse, Piet Mondrian and Ellsworth Kelly. His print *Yellow Iris, June 1, 1982* shares his elders' concern with line, but his heavy black drawings, at times quite sinister, are more massive and become, in the artist's words, "almost anti-flower." Their blackness represents a perverse denial of color, one of the flower's most distinguishing characteristics. They are strongly anthropomorphic, embracing both masculine and feminine sensibilities. For the artist, the tulip drawings, which number more than fifty, provide further commentary on the industrialization of contemporary society. The medium enables Sultan to contrast the delicate, natural form of the flower with the smoky, industrial quality of the charcoal.

In view of Sultan's strong interest in industrial processes, it is natural that he is drawn to printmaking; he has published a total of thirty thus far. The four aquatints in the 1983 *Black Tulips* series come directly out of the charcoal drawings and have the same smoldering borders, though they are considerably more abstract. Aquatint, a powder like charcoal, proved the perfect medium for translating the drawings into prints. His novel method of working—moving the powder around by blowing on it *before* it is heated—resulted in a

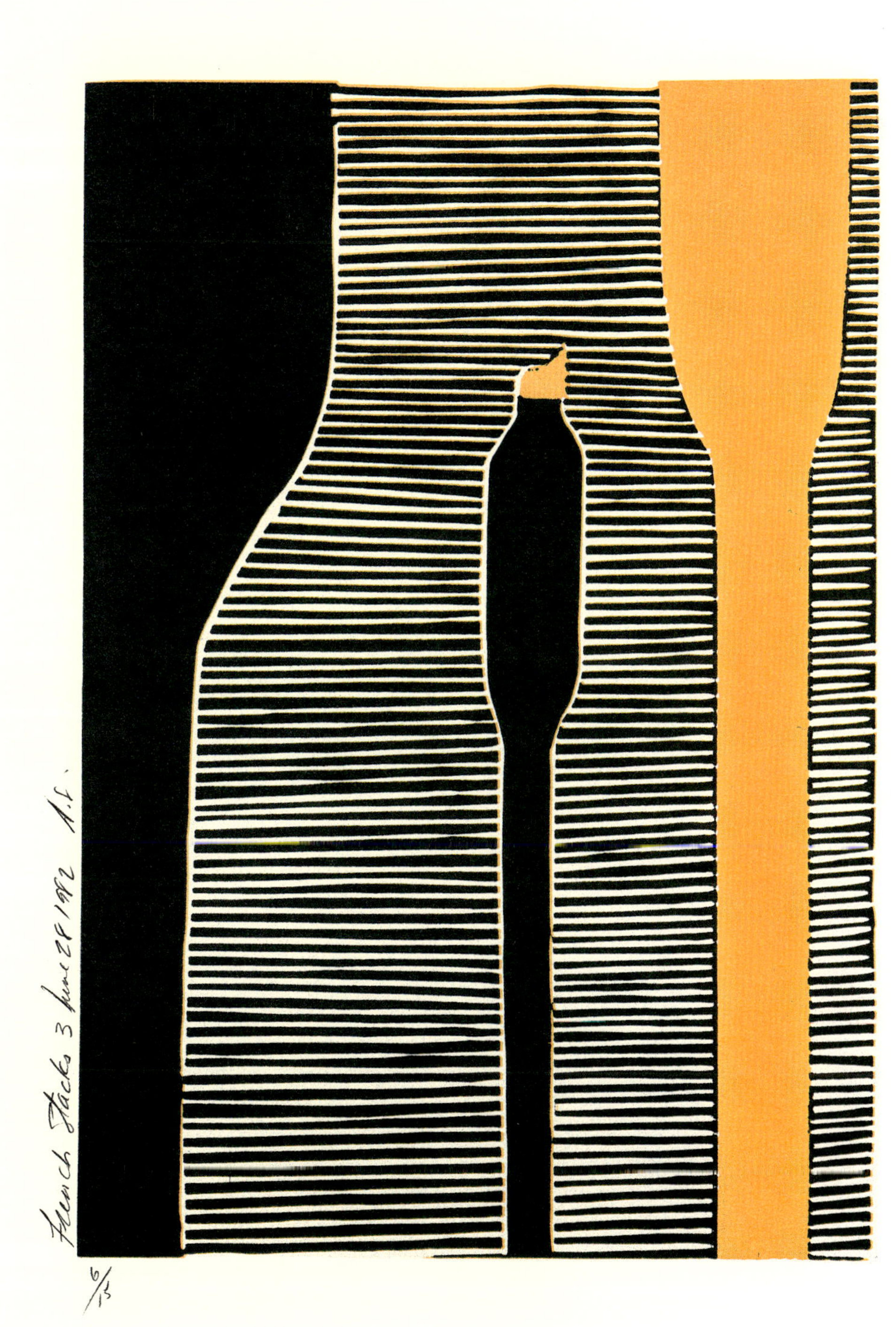

149. *French Stacks 3* 1982

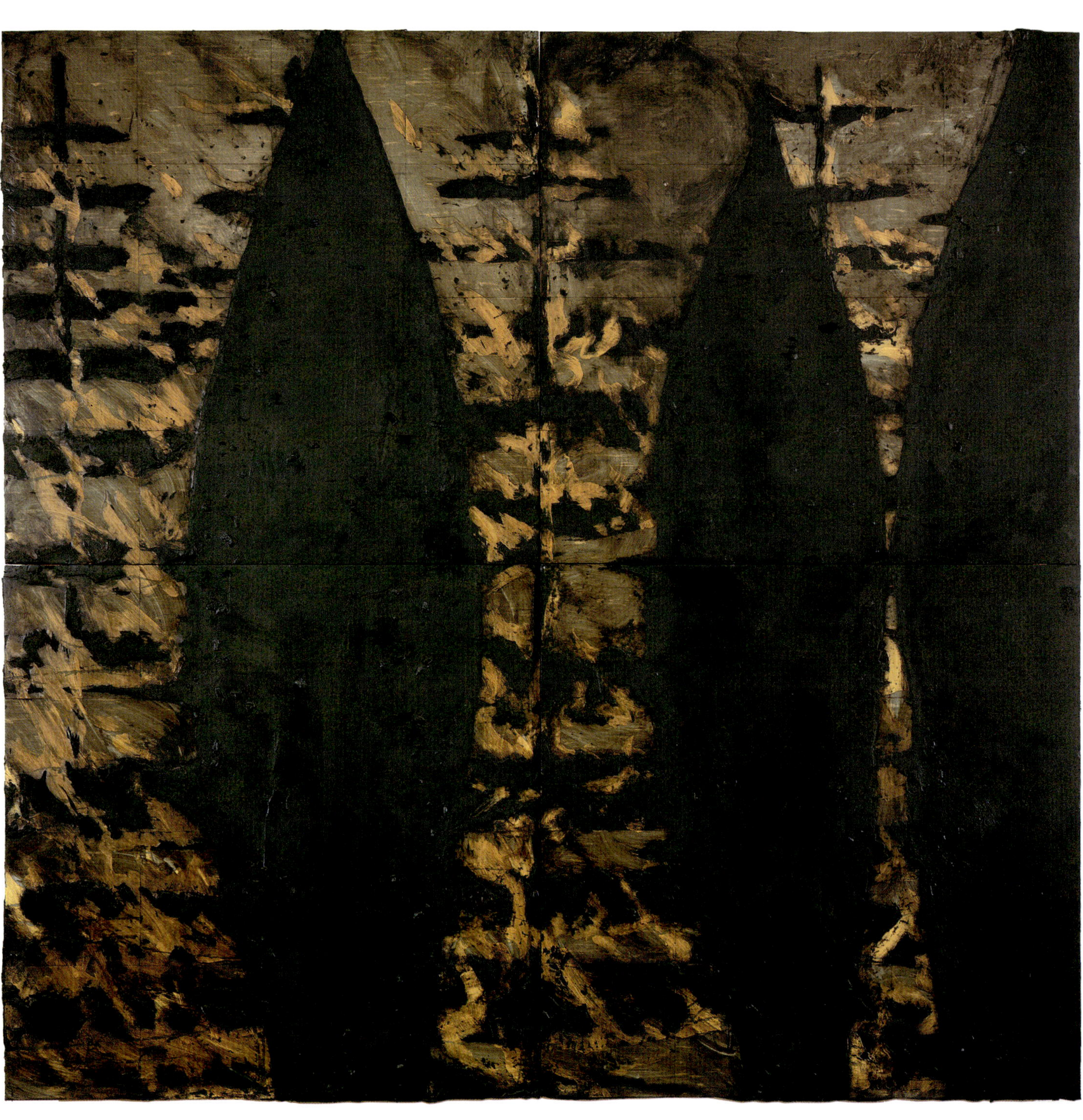

140. *Forest Fire, April 13, 1984*

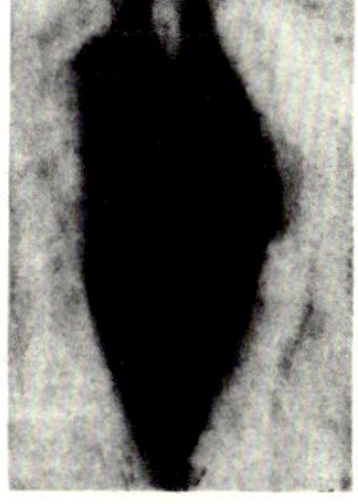

series of marvelously dreamlike and mysterious images, identifiable as tulips largely by the artist's titles scrawled along the right margin of the paper.

Forest Fire, April 13, 1984 (no. 140) is one of Sultan's most gestural paintings; its flames recall the work of Clyfford Still, one of the masters of Abstract Expressionism. Not surprisingly, the fire and light theme has previously made its appearance in a variety of guises, from smokestacks to cigarettes to streetlamps, and the haunting black presences of the trees evoke the black tulip forms as well. Unlike the almost geometric yellow flame that emerges from the smokestack and brings to mind a flower, these flames rage across the picture plane in uncontrollable fashion, suggesting a painting that verges on self-destruction. In both literal and figurative terms, Sultan pushes to an extreme the tension between structure (the trees) and gesture (the flames) in painting.

Sultan's powerful images chronicle the industrial era in its fading moments. He presents both sides of the coin: the excitement and glory as well as the unfulfilled promise of the time. In both his paintings and works on paper, Sultan accomplishes this by capturing the precise moment at which any one form reveals the greatest number of contradictions and possibilities.   MG

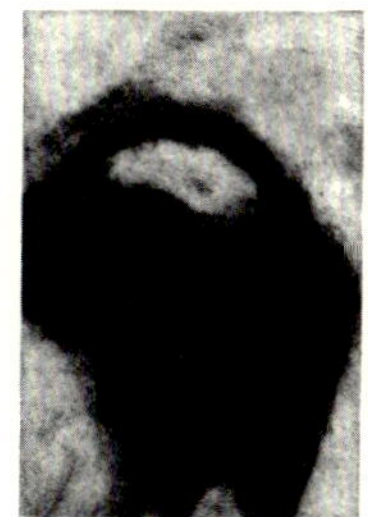

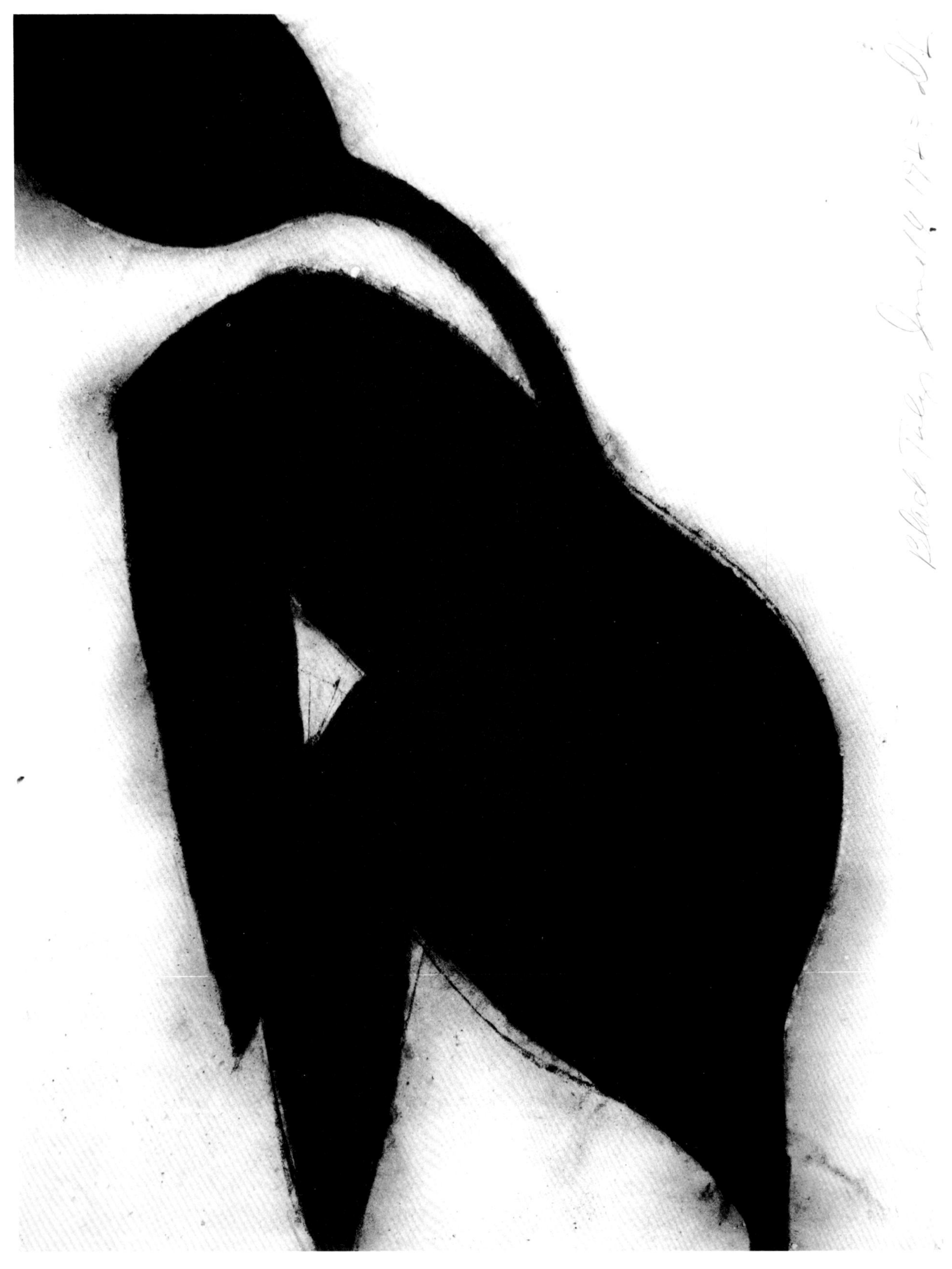

142. *Black Tulip, June 14, 1983*